1. Stewart Thompson showing off his 'sunday' jumper, knitted by his wife, Mrs Annie Thompson in the natural undyed colours of their own sheep.

a practical handbook
of traditional designs

FAIR ISLE
KNITTING

Sarah Don

MILLS & BOON LTD
London · Sydney · Toronto

Dedicated to Emily

Acknowledgement

My thanks to everyone on Fair Isle who gave us their
kind hospitality and help in our research, Alan, Annie,
Charles and Judy for their hard work and encouragement.

First published 1979

Reprinted 1980

© Sarah Don 1979

ISBN 0263 06383 6

Filmset and printed in Great Britain by
BAS Printers Limited, Over Wallop, Hampshire
and bound by Hunter & Foulis Ltd, Edinburgh
for the Publishers, Mills & Boon Ltd,
17–19 Foley Street, London W1A 1DR

Contents

The Origins and Development of Fair Isle Knitting

Fair Isle

'A bright green spot like an emerald on the wide ocean, this place is quite a little world in itself; covered with grass of a most vivid luxuriant verdure.'

The words of Catherine Sinclair in her book, *Shetland and the Shetlanders* (1840), are a perfect description of our first sight of this beautiful island. Fair Isle is one of the 100 Shetland Islands and the most isolated of the 20 which are inhabited. There are several possible Norse translations: 'Farey' meaning Sheep Isle, 'Fara', the fair Isle and 'Foer' meaning far off or distant.

Although the island lies on the same latitude as Greenland the winters are less severe than those of Scotland due to the passing Gulf Stream. The surrounding waters are treacherous but the island is well equipped with two lighthouses to warn the passing ships of the very real danger. Jerry Eunson's book, *The Shipwrecks of Fair Isle* tells us that 88 vessels have been wrecked or sunk since 900 AD; but how many more have gone unrecorded?

We set out for Fair Isle on 'The Good Shepherd', a 46ft cruiser that delivers visitors, supplies and mail to the island twice a week. My husband gave up trying to take pictures after the first half hour, and joined me for the remainder of the 3 hour crossing clinging to the winch in front of the wheel house. Although the crew assured us that our crossing had been 'quite calm' we made the return journey by air – a trip lasting 10 minutes!

Fair Isle varies in colour through the four seasons with flowering blue squills, red and white campion, roseroof willow and scurvy grass, with carpets of sea pinks. The heather-covered moors look wild and only the Great Skuas have made their homes here. The adults continue to make ferocious 'dive bomb' attacks on intruders, even after the young birds have left the nests.

As well as the many birds which inhabit the island

2. Looking out to Sheep Rock, Fair Isle's most valuable piece of grazing land once kept exclusively for moorit sheep is now home for one ram and a few sheep.

9

there is a large population of rabbits and its increase has become a matter of some concern for the islanders. Grazing land is precious and the question of whether or not the rabbits are putting as much back into the soil as they have taken out is one for careful consideration. The only other wild mammal is the island's own variety of mouse, 'The Fair Isle Mouse'.

Since Fair Isle was bought by the National Trust in 1954 the living conditions have been greatly improved. Electricity and sanitation have been provided but it is unfortunate that this restoration has demanded the sacrifice of some of the traditional characteristics of the buildings. Two of the old structures which remain are the churches, housing the two faiths: Church of Scotland and Methodist. It is a strongly religious community and this has been connected with the knitting craft of the island:

'Spiritual men and women, working together to produce the religious symbols and abstract forms, come nearer to their one God and closer together in their community.'
   H. E. Kiewe's book, *The Sacred History of Knitting*

Although the Shetland Isles have been part of Scotland for the last 500 years the people are more like the Norwegians in appearance, having fair hair and tanned skin. They speak with a very gentle accent, unlike that of the Scots, and their speech still includes much Norse.

During the 18th and 19th centuries there was much suffering under the tyrannical Scottish landlords. The people were paid less than two shillings for each 100 cwt of fish which was sold at a vast profit by the landlords on the Scottish market. In desperation they tried to sail or row their small boats across the dangerous waters to get a better price for their fish and to sell their knitting.

Beginnings

Although one of the earliest woollen garments found dates back to the 6th century BC, it is possible that knitting began even earlier than this as there is strong evidence to show that sheep were domesticated as early as 10,000 BC.

The earliest piece of knitting to bear any resemblance to Fair Isle designs is a pair of knitted patterned socks, found in a 4th century BC Egyptian tomb. However, it is generally thought that these were made in India for export to Egypt as the patterns are similar to Indian cotton prints from the same period.

3. Jimmy Stout walking over the more fertile grassy slopes at the southern end of the Island.

The great traders of the world at this time were the Arabs, travelling east to Tibet and west to Spain and other Mediterranean ports. It is thought that Arabian knitting must have influenced the multicoloured Spanish and Florentine silks of the 12th – 16th centuries. Patterns and fabrics similar to those of Fair Isle can still be found among the Basques in Northern Spain.

There is a popular belief that sailors from the ship 'El Gran Griffon', wrecked off Fair Isle during the Spanish Armada in 1588 brought the art of patterned knitting to the island. The 300 men stranded on Fair Isle spent seven weeks under dreadful conditions of cold and hunger. This makes it somewhat hard to imagine the convivial meetings of the Spaniards and the Islanders discussing knitting patterns and methods of dyeing wool. However, it is possible that a few Spaniards settled on the island, so passing on the 'moorish' influences to the Fair Isle designs and the methods of making fast dyes from the native plants and lichens.

Another popular theory is that the Norsemen brought the art of patterned knitting with them.

However, Faroese patterns are heavier and geometrically constructed, bearing more resemblance to Norwegian and Scandinavian designs. Fair Isle designs are

4. Shearing Fair Isle sheep in the early years of this century.

composed of ancient religious and national symbols intertwined with varied bands of delicate patterning. There are about 160 different designs and no individual pattern is ever repeated on the same garment, each band of patterning being different in some way.

When I visited Fair Isle, I took with me a sample knitted in a design from a 12th century Egyptian sock. I left it with Mrs. Annie Thompson who liked it so much that she said she would work it into one of her 'all over' jumpers. Mrs. Thompson pointed out that it could, in a few years time, become a 'traditional' Fair Isle design! (This sample is shown on page 12). The sample bears an incredible resemblance in its basic construction to a number of existing traditional Fair Isle designs also shown in this book.

Rise in Popularity

Wool has always been one of Fair Isle's most important natural resources. By the 16th century the knitted garments had become the main item of barter and the demand has been sustained throughout the years.

It was Elizabeth I of England who first encouraged knitting as a pastime for women. In 1589, when William Lee invented the first knitting machine, the men gave up hand knitting altogether and since then it has been a

5. Shetland women carding and spinning wool, mid-nineteenth century.

female-dominated occupation.

Shetland knitwear was first marketed in London in 1839 and by the middle of that century the cardigans made from natural undyed wools were popular with the clergy and were recommended by the medical profession, indeed Fair Isle designs have often been promoted by royalty. The Prince of Wales (later Edward VIII) wore a Fair Isle pullover whilst playing golf at St. Andrews in 1921.

Now there are only five women left on Fair Isle who still knit, and only Mrs. Annie Thompson knits the 'all over' jumpers. Since the war, very few girls were born to the islanders, but happily, in the last few years their number has increased and the women are confident that their craft will survive. When there are, once again, enough lichens and plants growing on the island, the women are keen to re-establish the art of dyeing their own wool.

6. The inside of a typical shetland croft in the nineteenth century.

Knitting machines were introduced to the Shetlands in 1930 but Fair Isle designs cannot be satisfactorily produced on machines and they continue to be made by hand. Many of the factories in England and Scotland ceased production of woollens during the War and this proved to be a time of great prosperity for the islanders as the women found value for money when they bought Fair Isle jumpers with their clothing coupons.

Fair Isle garments are as popular as ever and the increasing fame and excellent quality of the goods means that production will never be able to meet the vast demand.

Wool

There have been sheep on the Shetland Isles since prehistoric Stone Age man. The long dark winters, bitter wind and poor pastures meant that only the hardiest animals could survive.

A number of sheep plus one ram are kept on top of Sheep Rock which is a remarkable piece of grazing land nearly 400ft high and about 10 acres in size. This is the best pasture on the Island, due to the shelter provided by the sloping land, and the upward deflection of the winds impinging on the straight cliffs of the craig. Up to the middle of the 17th century access was by junction with the land which has since fallen away, now the men climb

7. The much-disputed label for knitted garments made in Shetland. Fair Isle's label reads: 'Fair Isle made in Fair Isle'.

8. Carding, spinning and knitting, Fair Isle c 1920.

15

to the top by way of a fixed chain and hoist the sheep up after them.

Over the centuries evolved the finest, softest sheep's wool found anywhere in the world and until 50 years ago all of it was spun by hand by the women. It was teased and then oiled with fish oil (kreesh) and rolled into small balls ready for spinning. Today, however, all the wool is spun on the mainland.

Until a few years ago, the women dyed their own wool, using the cherished secret methods of making fast dyes from the Island's native flowers, leaves, roots and lichens. now there are not enough ingredients left to continue dyeing so the garments are made in the natural colours of the Island's Shetland sheep – soft brown from the Moorit sheep, black from the Black sheep, natural white, grey and fawn, and a beautiful pinky beige, which is a mixture of moorit and white.

Practical Guidelines

The layouts in this book are designed to be as clear and simple as possible. The charts relate to the photograph, key and list of colours accompanying each chart so that all the necessary information can be viewed together.

One of the first pullovers I made was for a friend's two year old son and this didn't take too long to complete. After this I had gained enough confidence to make one for my husband. I was now addicted! My third was comfortably finished within two weeks.

Once you have knitted the first half of your garment you will find that you know the design almost by heart! Some people remember the designs in a series of numbers eg. $1 - 3 - 5 - 3 - 1$ etc. Others remember by 'seeing' shapes eg. lines, squares, triangles, diamonds etc. Either way you must remember that each stitch in each colour, and each group of stitches in any one colour relates to the one above, below and to either side.

Fortunately, Fair Isle knitting is not as complicated as it may seem, but if, when you first start, you find you are getting a little confused then study the photograph and chart further. You will probably find that you have made a mistake. Do undo a few rows if this is the case. If you leave it, the whole progress of the design will be disrupted and just won't make sense.

At first you will have to concentrate very hard, so set aside a few quiet evenings at home. After a while it will become easier and you will be able to listen to the radio or watch the television at the same time.

One word of warning! Try not to boast too much about all your hard work or you will find yourself knitting for all your family and friends!

How to use the charts
Each symbol represents a colour as indicated in the key. Work from top to bottom, (including motifs or symbols which are placed 'upside down' on the chart).

When knitting on the round, the total number of stitches used is an exact multiple of all repeat nos. of the patterns used and the following instructions will not be necessary.

Opposite the chart are details of the repeats. Some designs have bands of patterning with different numbers of stitches in their repeats, you will have to deal with these separately.

Follow this procedure carefully:

1. Count the number of stitches you intend to use before beginning the patterning. If this number is an exact multiple of the number of stitches to the repeat you will be able to knit from end to end of the chart exactly.

2. If this is not so divide the repeat number into the number of stitches you are using.
   eg. repeat over 8 sts – 37 sts on needle:

$$\begin{array}{r} \underline{4} \text{ times repeat} + 5 \text{ sts} \\ 8 \overline{\smash{)}37} \\ \underline{32} \\ 5 \end{array}$$

   This means you will knit the whole repeat four times with five stitches left over.

3. Draw a line in pencil between fifth and sixth stitches in, from left side of chart.

4. First row: Begin at first stitch on left side of chart. Work to the right across the whole repeat four times, then knit last five stitches as first five stitches from left side of start, ending row at the fifth stitch.

5. Second row: Begin row with the fifth stitch. Work back to left side of chart (five stitches), go to right side of chart and work across four whole repeats (last stitch will be first stitch on left side of chart). Repeat these two rows throughout the design.

You will find this whole process of where to begin and end unnecessary as you become familiar with the design. You should also remember that any change in the number of stitches on your needle will also change where you begin and end the patterning.

Colours

If you decide to choose your own colour scheme, try not to pick too many – and make sure that each colour does not react badly to any of the others (eg. bright green and lemon yellow would be seen for miles, bright green and bright pink would be blinding). Two light colours of the same tone could become indistinguishable when knitted together – pale olive green and pale blue, or pink and beige.

Every design has dark and light colours in certain areas and if these are changed around a completely different, although sometimes a very exciting, result emerges.

A good method of choosing your colour scheme is to find two colours of the same tone that you like together. Then find the same two colours in a lighter or darker shade. Choose a fifth colour that contrasts with the other four, and of course a base colour. You can use varying shades through the bands of patterns to provide more depth and interest.

Repeat numbers

All the designs repeat over a set number of stitches and the exact size of the main body piece largely depends on this repeat number. All the designs that are to be used must repeat exactly all the way around to avoid an ugly seam at the beginning and end of each round. However, this does not apply when knitting the sleeves due to the number of decreases down to the cuffs.

The number of stitches used for the main body piece must be an exact multiple of all the different repeat numbers of the designs you wish to knit. For example:

A = 6 sts
B = 28 sts
C = 24 sts
D = 24 sts

The tension is 9 sts to 2.5cms (1in), and the size required is to fit 91.5 – 96.5 cms (36 – 38ins). The ideal total number of sts would be 9×37ins = 333 sts (chest measurement).

Pattern A   =   6 sts $\times$ 56 = 336
Pattern B   = 28 sts $\times$ 12 = 336
Patterns C & D = 24 sts $\times$ 14 = 336

336 is, therefore, an exact multiple of all the above repeat numbers and is a satisfactory total.

336 sts divided by 9 sts to 1in = 37.3ins.

If one or more of the repeat numbers does not wholly divide into a satisfactory total, you will have to make a compromise. Either change the needle size or change the design slightly, by either taking away or adding stitches to the design, preferably in the spaces on the base colour, so increasing or decreasing the repeat number.

Knitting on the round

The women of Fair Isle and Shetland still use the ancient method of knitting in rounds, with up to five needles at a time, and with the help of a knitting belt or pouch.

Christ's seamless robe, for which the soldiers cast lots, would have been made in this way, as were the Egyptian/Arabian socks of 4,000 BC.

All the garments are made completely seamless in a very simple way, considering the complicated patterns. Basically a jumper is made cylindrical up to the shoulders, folded flat, and the shoulders grafted together either side to the neck. The armholes are cut, turned under and sewn. Another more efficient way is to wrap all yarns in use on each round, around the needle 10 or 12 times where you wish to divide for the armholes to be dropped. This procedure is repeated on every following round. When the body piece is completed to the shoulders, the loops are then cut, tied and sewn in to the back of the fabric for approximately 2.5cms (1in). The same procedure applies for the front openings of cardigans and jackets.

I have combined both ancient and modern methods, the main body piece being knitted on the round to the base of the armhole, then knitting front and back separately, in rows. However, this is just my personal preference and you can experiment to see which method you will find most efficient.

The sleeves are made by picking up and knitting stitches from around the armhole onto the required number of needles and knitting down to the cuff, gradually decreasing to the required number of stitches.

There is a triangular gusset incorporated into the sleeve at the base of the armhole to create a more comfortable fit.

General hints for knitting on the round
a) When using a circular needle, or more than the two needles quoted in most of the patterns, tie a coloured thread to the last and centre stitch cast on to mark the end of round and 'side-seam'.

b) A loop of yarn in contrasting colour should be placed on the right-hand needle at the end of the first round. It is slipped onto the right-hand needle, moving up with the work, at the end of every round, thus making a convenient marker loop for the end of each round. Be careful not to knit this into the fabric.

c) When using a set of double-ended needles, take care to knit the first and last stitch on every needle fairly tightly to avoid an ugly seam down the fabric. When using Shetland wool you will have to be careful not to knit too tightly, however, as the soft yarn is liable to break.

d) When knitting on the round, every round is knitted as the right side is outside and facing you. This also helps when knitting coloured patterns, making it easier to follow the designs as you work. Unless given specific instructions to the contrary, stocking stitch is produced by knitting every round.

e) Avoid joining new balls of yarn anywhere except at the end of the round. A rough calculation of how much yarn you will need to complete a round would be to multiply the length of the round by three.

Circular needles

Circular needles or 'twin pins' are made in different lengths and sizes and consist of two short needles joined by a thin wire flex. They can also be used for knitting in rows, turning at each end, knitting backwards and forwards. The only disadvantage of using twin pins is that you cannot use them for smaller garments such as gloves and mittens, as the total number of stitches must be large enough to go all the way round the twin pin, from point to point without stretching the fabric. Double-ended needles are used for knitting sleeves.

When buying a twin pin the assistant will, with the aid of a chart and details of the yarn and number of stitches used, help you to find needles of an appropriate length.

Circular knitting on three or more needles

This requires a number of double-ended needles of appropriate size and length, plus another to knit with. Most of the instructions in this book require two 41cm (16in) needles plus one to knit with. If you cannot obtain these long needles, or you prefer to knit with more, divide the total number of stitches to be cast on by the number of needles you wish to use. This will give the number of stitches to be cast on to each needle. The remainder of the instructions will be quite straightforward, but you must repeat this calculation when you pick up and knit stitches for the sleeves and neck shaping. Begin knitting with the spare needle and the first stitch on the first needle.

The knitting belt

This is a belt worn around the waist with the pouch resting on the right hip at the front. The pouch is oval shaped and stuffed with horse hair and has holes large enough to hold the stationary needle, so supporting the weight of the garment and freeing the right hand for mixing colours, and controlling the tension. The speed is greatly increased and some women reach speeds of up to 200 stitches per minute.

As the work grows, it is attached to the left hip by means of a safety pin and loops of yarn thus enabling the knitter to drop her work at any time as it is held by the needle in the pouch and the safety pin.

Stranding

Knit the required number of stitches in first colour. Drop the first colour, place right-hand needle into first stitch of second colour, but don't knit yet; *gently but firmly pull back the last 10 or 12 stitches knitted along the right-hand needle so that your work is slightly stretched.* Now take up 2nd colour and knit the next set of stitches. Repeat this process every time you change colour.

This method of stranding is preferable to weaving as it produces a less dense and softer fabric, but must only be used for groups of 5 stitches or less. For a larger number of stitches in any one colour you must 'weave in' on every third stitch.

'Weaving in'

Knit the first stitch in first colour, place 2nd colour over 1st colour, knit the next stitch, bring the 2nd colour back over the 1st colour. Proceding in this way the yarn is woven into the back of the work without being seen on the right side.

To weave in the ends

When breaking and joining new colours at the beginning and end of the round/row leave about 6ins of spare yarn. Join the new colour and the discarded colour with a single knot, at the same time easing the yarn through the first and last few stitches of the round to an even tension. Begin the next round and weave the spare yarn into the first 8–10 stitches of the round. Carefully cut away the excess.

Tensions

Your tension should be measured over both patterned and plain stocking stitch over squares of at least 10cms

(4ins). Count the number of stitches per 2.5cms (1in). If your tension measures different to that quoted use smaller or larger needles accordingly.

If you intend to use a circular pin for your garment use the twin pin for the tension square.

When you have completed your garment, carefully measure across the chest. Find the total number of stitches used at this point and divide this number by the number of cms/ins. This will give you a highly accurate figure for the number of stitches per cm/inch. Make a note of this figure, the yarn and needle sizes for future use.

Shetland 2-ply jumper yarn (knits as 4-ply)
Over patterning in stocking stitch:
3mm (no. 11) needles: 9 sts to 2.5cm (1in).
3¼mm (no. 10) needles: 8.4 sts to 2.5cm (1in).
Over plain stocking stitch:
3¼mm (no. 10) needles: 7.25 sts to 2.5cm (1in).
3mm (no. 11) needles: 8.13 sts to 2.5cm (1in).
2¾mm (no. 12) needles: 9 sts to 2.5cm (1in).

Yarns

All of the garments and samples shown have been knitted in T. M. Hunter's Shetland 2-ply jumper yarn, which knits up as 4-ply. This yarn can be obtained by post (see list of suppliers). However, if you decide to use a different yarn there are many others available, although the majority will contain only a small percentage of Shetland wool.

Don't be tempted to use a cheap yarn in order to save money. As you've taken so much trouble making your garment it's worthwhile buying a really good yarn that will last longer and feel much softer. If you use a different yarn to the one quoted, you must follow the instructions concerning tension very carefully.

After-care

Shetland Wool and Pure Wool Yarns
Follow the manufacturer's instructions, but in general these yarns should *not* be pressed, machine washed or spun. Hand wash in warm soap suds, rinse well, gently wring and dry flat away from direct heat. In Fair Isle and Shetland, garments are dried on wooden frames or 'stretchers', which greatly help to keep the garment's shape.

Mixtures, Nylon and Synthetics
Again, follow the manufacturer's instructions. If you intend to dry knitted garments out of doors, turn them inside out to prevent the colours fading.

Sizes

The size of the garment should be based on your chest measurement and, in general, the garment should be the same size across the chest as your own chest measurement. However, if you prefer a looser fitting garment you should make it 2ins larger than your own chest measurement.

Garments such as the Lady's Jacket and Yoked Cardigan and the Fisherman's Jumper require slightly more width across the chest and sleeves.

If you wish to design your own garments you will have to take into account the style, and button bands etc., and most important, your yarn and tension.

Fitting

After finding the correct tension and choosing your size take the trouble to constantly measure and try on your garment as you would if you were dressmaking (place stitches on pins or holders or onto a contrasting coloured yarn). There are a number of places where you should try on the garment and check the measurements:

1. A few cms above the ribbing or hem.
2. Just before you divide for the front, back and armholes (to check for length).
3. Before dividing for neck shaping (for length of armhole).
4. Before ending at shoulders.
5. Before any neck ribbing, collars etc.
6. After first 15cms (6ins) of the first sleeve (to check width of the sleeve).
7. At the end of the sleeve (to check for length).

Grafting

Method A
Remove sts from needles. Place fabric on a flat surface, right side up with the two lines of sts together. Using base colour and blunt needle begin at right edge. Pass needle up through first st of bottom piece and up through next st on left at bottom.

*Go back to first st at top and pass needle down

through it and back up through next st to the left at top. Return to bottom piece and pass needle down through last st it came up through. Bring up through next st on left and the bottom. Pull yarn to the correct tension. Repeat from * to end. Weave in ends for 6 sts at back of work.

Method B

Leave sts on needles, place right sides together (unless otherwise stated). With sts evenly spread on needles, using base colour and 3rd knitting needle knit first st on front needle and first st on back needle together onto 3rd needle. Knit 2nd st of front needle and 2nd st of back needle together onto 3rd needle. Pull 1st st knitted over 2nd st knitted so casting off 1st st. Repeat until all sts are cast off.

Abbreviations

K	=	knit
P	=	purl
st(s)	=	stitch(es)
st st	=	stocking stitch
rep	=	repeat
beg	=	begin(ning)
dec	=	decrease
inc	=	increase
tbl	=	through back of loop
sl	=	slip
psso	=	pass slip stitch over
tog	=	together
ins	=	inches
cms	=	centimetres
mm	=	millimetres
nos	=	numbers
cont	=	continue
col	=	colour
rem	=	remain(ing)
foll	=	following
alt	=	alternate

Needle sizes

English Size	Metric	American
000	9.00	15
00	8.50	13
0	8.00	12
1	7.50	11
2	7.00	$10\frac{1}{2}$
3	6.50	10
4	6.00	9
5	5.50	8
6	5.00	7
7	4.50	6
8	4.00	5
9	3.50	4
10	3.25	3
11	3.00	2
12	2.50	1
13	2.25	0
14	2.00	00

Equivalents

1in	=	2.5cms (25mm)
1oz	=	28 grammes

Sample 1

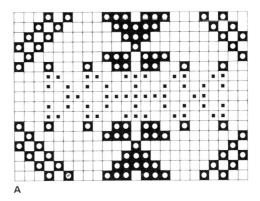

A

B

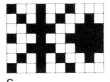

C

D

Shetland 2-ply jumper yarn
black, (5); red (43); blue (FC41); cream
(1a) (base colour).

Repeats
A 24 sts; B 4 sts; C 10 sts; D 4 sts.

Pattern order
* B, C, D, A, (rep from *).
5 plain rows base colour between each
band of patterning.

⊡	Red (43)
■	Black (5)
▪	Blue (FC41)
☐	Cream (1a)(Base Colour)

Sample 2

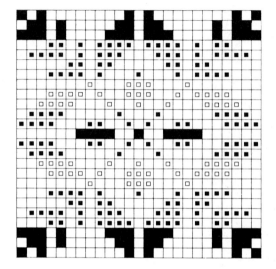

Shetland 2-ply jumper yarn
cream (1a); base colour; black (5); blue
(21); light blue (33).

Repeats
Over 25 sts and 25 rows.

■ Black (5)

▪ Blue (21)

▫ Light Blue (33)

☐ Cream (1a)

Sample 3

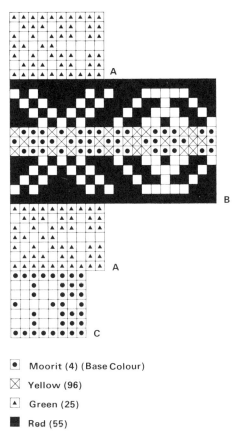

Shetland 2-ply jumper yarn

green (25); cream (1a); red (55); moorit (4)
(base colour); pale yellow (96).

Repeats
A 10 sts; B 22 sts; C 8 sts.

Pattern order
* A, B, A, C, (rep from *).

● Moorit (4) (Base Colour)
⊠ Yellow (96)
▲ Green (25)
■ Red (55)
☐ Cream (1a)

Sample 4

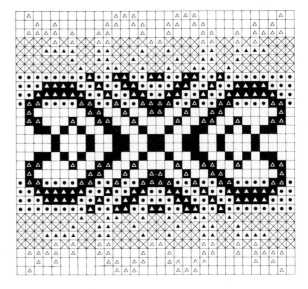

Shetland 2-ply jumper yarn
green (25); cream (1a); pale green (26);
med. green (47); olive green (83); dark
green (34): apricot (53); yellow (66).

Repeats
Over 30 stitches and 30 rows.

■	Dark Green (34)
△	Olive Green (83)
▲	Med. Green (47)
◤	Green (25)
◁	Pale Green (26)
⊡	Apricot (53)
⊠	Yellow (66)
☐	Cream (1a)

Sample 5

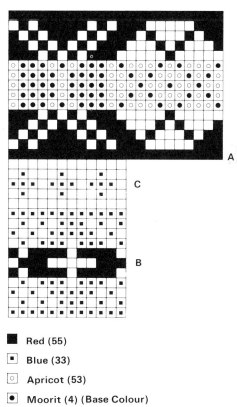

Shetland 2-ply jumper yarn
red (55); cream (1a); apricot (53); moorit
(4) (base colour); blue (33).

Repeats
A 22 sts; B 12 sts; C 4 sts.

Pattern order
* C, B, C, A, (rep from *).

■ Red (55)

▪ Blue (33)

◦ Apricot (53)

● Moorit (4) (Base Colour)

☐ Cream (1a)

Sample 6

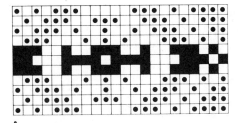

A

B

C

B

- ● Moorit (4)
- □ Cream (1a)
- ■ Black (5) (Base Colour)
- ⊙ Fawn (78)

Shetland 2-ply jumper yarn
black (5) (base colour); fawn (78); cream
(1a); moorit (4).

Repeats
A 22 sts; B 4 sts; C 10 sts.

Pattern order
* A, B, C, B, (rep from *).
4 plain rows between each band of
patterning.

Sample 7

Shetland 2-ply jumper yarn
blue (33); Grey (203) (base colour); black
(5); cream (1a); yellow (96); rust (FC38).

Repeats
A 34 sts; B 8 sts; C 16 sts.

Pattern order
* B, C, B, A, (rep from *).
2 rows of black between each band of
patterning.

- ▪ Blue (33)
- ◨ Rust (FC38)
- ⊠ Yellow (96)
- ■ Black (5)
- □ Cream (1a)
- ⊡ Grey (203) (Base Colour)

Sample 8

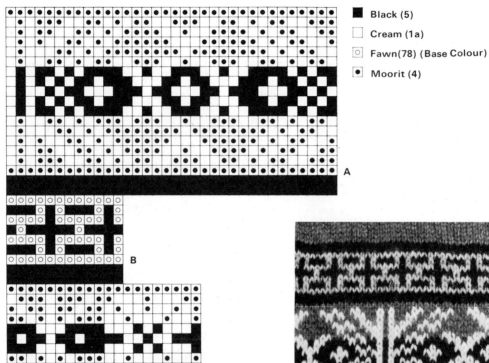

- ■ Black (5)
- □ Cream (1a)
- ⊙ Fawn(78) (Base Colour)
- ● Moorit (4)

A

B

C

Shetland 2-ply jumper yarn
cream (1a); moorit (4); black (5); fawn (78) (base colour).

Repeats
A 34 sts; B 6 sts; C 20 sts.

Pattern order
* B, C, B, A, (rep from *).
2 rows black over each band of patterning.

Sample 9

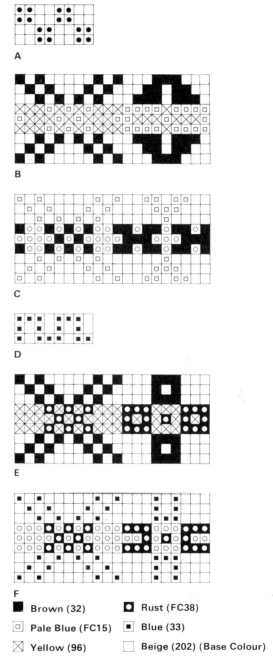

A

B

C

D

E

F

Shetland 2-ply jumper yarn
moorit (4); brown (32); yellow (96); pale
blue (FC15); beige (202) (base colour);
dark blue (33); apricot (53); rust (FC38).

Repeats

A 4 sts; B 20 sts; C 20 sts; D 4 sts; E 20 sts;
F 20 sts.

Pattern order

* A, B, A, C, D, E, D, F, (rep from *).
2 plain rows base colour between each
band of patterning.

■ Brown (32)   ▢ Rust (FC38)

▫ Pale Blue (FC15)   ■ Blue (33)

⊠ Yellow (96)   ▢ Beige (202) (Base Colour)

◯ Apricot (53)   ● Moorit (4)

Sample 10

Shetland 2-ply jumper yarn
grey (54); olive (83); dark apricot (207); med. apricot (53); pale yellow (96); cream (1a); fawn (78); light grey (2); sage green (29); beige (202) (base colour); black (5); moorit (4).

Repeats
Over 33 stitches and 28 rows.
All-over design repeating from side to side *and* top to bottom.

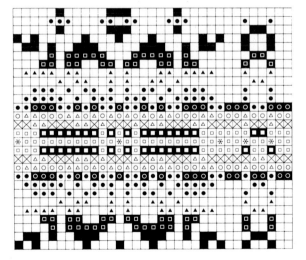

- ■ Light Grey (2)
- ✳ Fawn (78)
- △ Sage Green (29)
- ⊠ Pale Yellow (96)
- ○ Med. Apricot (53)
- • Moorit (4)
- ◉ Dark Apricot (207)
- ▲ Olive (83)
- ◨ Grey (54)
- ■ Black (5)
- ☐ Beige (202) (Base Colour)
- ▫ Cream (1a)

Sample 11

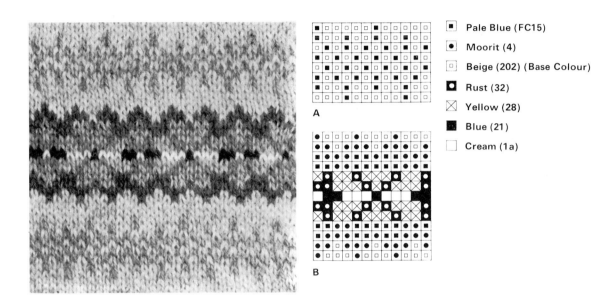

A

B

■	Pale Blue (FC15)
●	Moorit (4)
□	Beige (202) (Base Colour)
◨	Rust (32)
⊠	Yellow (28)
▨	Blue (21)
□	Cream (1a)

Shetland 2-ply jumper yarn
blue (FC15); moorit (4); beige (202) (base
colour); yellow (28): dark blue (21);
cream (1a); rust (32).

Repeats
A 6 sts; B 12 sts.

Pattern order
* A, B, (rep from *).
2 plain rows base colour between each
band of patterning.

Sample 12

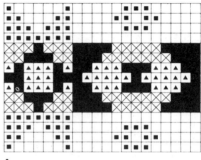

A

B

Shetland 2-ply jumper yarn
blue (33); yellow (FC40); green (25); black (5); beige (202) (base colour); rust (FC38).

Repeats
A 20 sts; B 5 sts.

Pattern order
* A, B, (rep from *).
3 plain rows base colour between each band of patterning.

▲	Green (25)
◉	Rust (FC38)
■	Blue (33)
⊠	Yellow (FC40)
□	Beige (202)
■	Black (5)

Sample 13

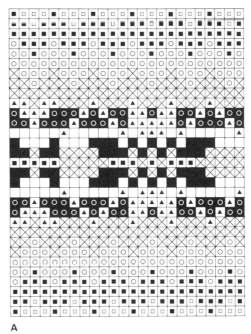

A

B

Shetland 2-ply jumper yarn
green (25); dark pink (FC33); rust
(FC38); pale pink (101); yellow (28); blue
(21); beige (202) (base colour); cream (1a).

Repeats
A 24 sts; B 8 sts.

Pattern order
* B, A, (rep from *).
3 plain rows base colour between each
band of patterning.

- ■ Blue (21)
- ■ Rust (FC38)
- ▫ Beige (202) (Base Colour)
- ⊠ Yellow (28)
- ▲ Green (25)
- ⊙ Pale Pink (101)
- ◉ Dark Pink (FC33)
- □ Cream (1a)

Sample 14

(Samples 14–17 are possibly from Indian patterned stockings found in Egypt.)

Shetland 2-ply jumper yarn
pale blue (33); dark blue (21); cream (base colour) (1a).

Repeats
A 20 sts; B 34 sts.

Pattern order
* A, B, (rep from *).
4 rows plain base colour between each band of patterning.

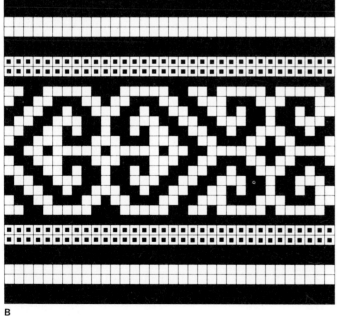

B

A

■ Pale Blue (33)

☐ Cream (1a) (Base Colour)

■ Blue (21)

Sample 15

Shetland 2-ply jumper yarn
dark blue (21); light blue (33); cream (1a)
(base colour).

Pattern
Repeat over 12 stitches.

■ Pale Blue (33)

☐ Cream (1a) (Base Colour)

■ Blue (21)

Sample 16

Shetland 2-ply jumper yarn
cream (1a) (base colour); blue (21); pale blue (33).

■ Blue (21)

▣ Pale Blue (33)

☐ Cream (1a) (Base Colour)

Sample 17

Sample 18

Shetland 2-ply jumper yarn
cream (1a) (base colour); pale blue (33);
dark blue (21).

Shetland 2-ply jumper yarn
brown (31); cream (1a) (base colour);
black (5); blue (FC41).

Repeats
A 4 sts; B 12 sts.

Pattern order
* A, B, (rep from *).
5 rows plain base colour between each
band of patterning.

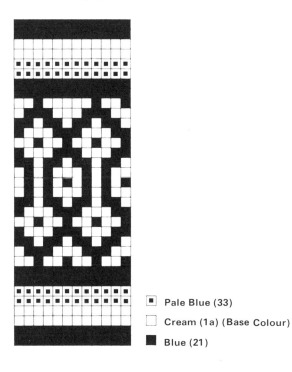

■ Pale Blue (33)

□ Cream (1a) (Base Colour)

■ Blue (21)

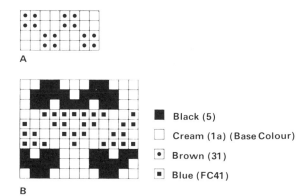

A

B

■ Black (5)

□ Cream (1a) (Base Colour)

• Brown (31)

■ Blue (FC41)

Sample 19

A

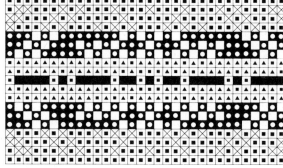

B

C

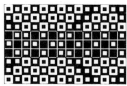

D

Shetland 2-ply jumper yarn
red (55); cream (1a); blue (FC41); yellow
(28); black (5); green (34); pink (78); grey
(203) base colour.

Repeats
A 8 sts; B 32 sts; C 8 sts; D 14 sts.

Pattern order
* A, B, C, D, (rep from *).
4 rows plain base colour between each
band of patterning.

■ Blue (FC41)

□ Grey (203) (Base Colour)

◘ Red (55)

■ Black (5)

▲ Green (34)

▪ Fawn (78)

⊠ Yellow (28)

□ Cream (1a)

Sample 20

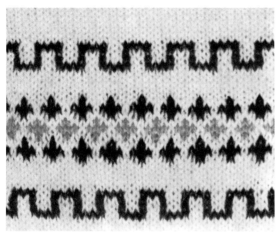

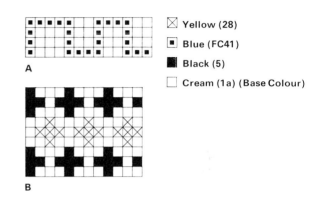

☒ Yellow (28)

▪ Blue (FC41)

■ Black (5)

☐ Cream (1a) (Base Colour)

A

B

Shetland 2-ply jumper yarn
blue (FC41); black (5); cream (1a) (base
colour); yellow (28).

Repeats
A 6 sts; B 4 sts.

Pattern order
* A, B, (rep from *).
5 rows base colour between each band of
patterning.

Sample 21

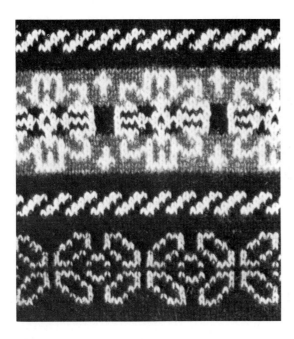

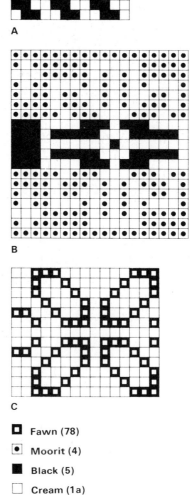

A

B

C

Shetland 2-ply jumper yarn
cream (1a); black (5) (base colour); moorit (4); fawn (78).

Repeats
A 4 sts; B 18 sts; C 15 sts.

Pattern order
* A, B, A, C, (rep from *).
4 rows plain base colour between each band of patterning.

☐ Fawn (78)

⊡ Moorit (4)

■ Black (5)

☐ Cream (1a)

Sample 22

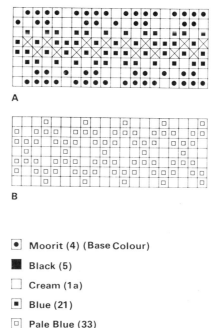

A

B

- ● Moorit (4) (Base Colour)
- ■ Black (5)
- □ Cream (1a)
- ▪ Blue (21)
- ▫ Pale Blue (33)
- ⊠ Yellow (66)

Shetland 2-ply jumper yarn

cream (1a); dark blue (21); yellow (66); black (5); blue (33); moorit (4); base colour.

Repeats

A 10 sts; B 4 sts; C 36 sts.

Pattern order

* A, B, C, B, (rep from *).
4 plain rows base colour between each band of patterning.

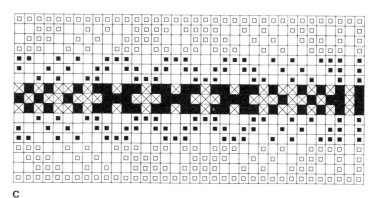

C

Sample 23

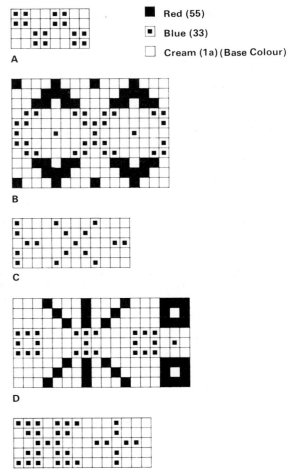

Red (55)

Blue (33)

Cream (1a) (Base Colour)

A

B

C

D

E

F

Shetland 2-ply jumper yarn
blue (33); cream (1a) (base colour); red (55).

Repeats
A 4 sts; B 8 sts; C 12 sts; D 18 sts; E 14 sts; F 18 sts.

Pattern order
* A, B, C, D, E, F, (rep from *).
4 plain rows base colour between each band of patterning.

48

Sample 24

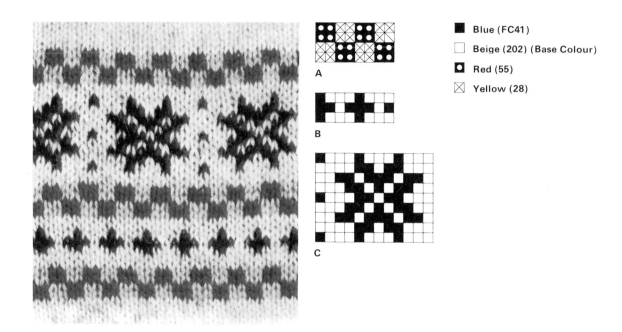

A

B

C

Blue (FC41)

Beige (202) (Base Colour)

Red (55)

Yellow (28)

Shetland 2-ply jumper yarn
blue (FC41); red (55); beige (202) (base colour); yellow (28).

Repeats
A 4 sts; B 4 sts; C 12 sts.

Pattern order
* A, B, A, C, (rep from *).
2 plain rows base colour between each band of patterning.

Sample 25

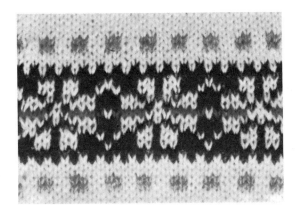

Shetland 2-ply jumper yarn
blue (21); red (55); green (25); cream (1a)
(base colour); grey (2); yellow (28).

Repeats
A 2 sts; B 12 sts.

Pattern order
* A, B, (rep from *).
2 plain rows base colour between each
band of patterning.

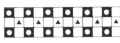

A

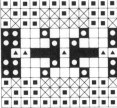

B

▲ Green (25)

■ Grey (2)

▪ Blue (21)

☒ Yellow (28)

◲ Red (55)

☐ Cream (1a) (Base Colour)

Sample 26

Shetland 2-ply jumper yarn
dark blue (FC41); blue (FC15); yellow
(66); orange (207); pale orange (53);
cream (1a); red (55).

Repeats
A 4 sts; B 12 sts.

Pattern order
* A, B, (rep from *).
2 plain rows base colour between each
band of patterning.

A

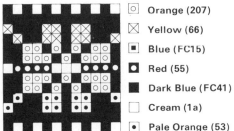

B

⊡ Orange (207)

☒ Yellow (66)

▪ Blue (FC15)

◲ Red (55)

■ Dark Blue (FC41)

☐ Cream (1a)

⊡ Pale Orange (53)

Sample 27

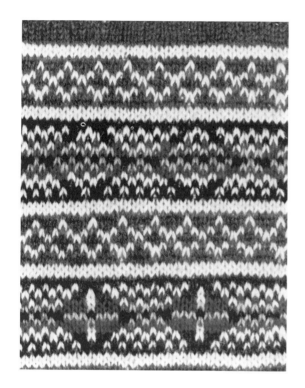

A

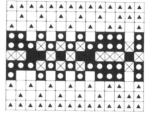

B

A

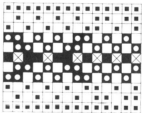

C

Shetland 2-ply jumper yarn
cream (1a); moorit (4) (base colour);
green (83); red (55); blue (21); black (5);
yellow (28).

Repeats
A 4 sts; B 14 sts; C 14 sts.

Pattern order
* A, B, A, C, (rep from *).
2 plain rows of cream between each band
of patterning.

- ■ Blue (2)
- ▲ Green (83)
- ⊠ Yellow (28)
- ⊙ Moorit (4) (Base Colour)
- ☐ Cream (1a)
- ■ Black (5)
- ◘ Red (55)

Sample 28

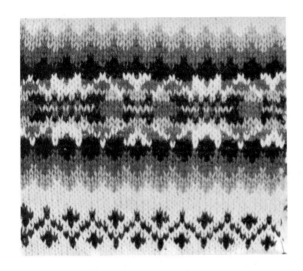

Shetland 2-ply jumper yarn
yellow (28); rust (FC38); blue (FC41);
cream (1a): base colour.

Repeats
A 24 sts; B 8 sts.

Pattern order
* A, B, (rep from *).
4 plain rows base colour between each
band of patterning.

A

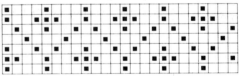

B

■ Blue (FC41)

■ Rust (FC38)

⊠ Yellow (28)

☐ Cream (1a) (Base Colour)

Lady's Round Neck Jumper

Shetland 2-ply jumper yarn
cream (1a), black (5), moorit (4).

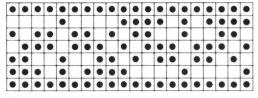

A

■ Black (5)

□ Cream (1a) (Base Colour)

⊡ Moorit (4)

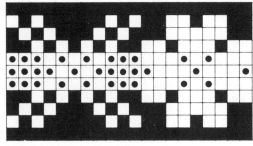

B

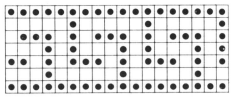

E

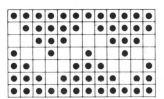

C

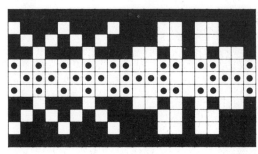

F

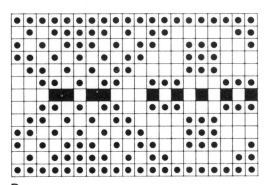

D

G

H

Repeats

A 20 sts; B 20 sts; C 6 sts; D 20 sts; E 6 sts; F 20 sts; G 12 sts; H 20 sts; I 4 sts; J 20 sts; K 10 sts; L 20 sts; M 8 sts; N 20 sts; O 8 sts.

Pattern Order

A through to O.

2 plain rows base colour between each band of patterning.

Sizes

Actual size 85(90:95.5:102)cms (33½:35½:37½:40ins).

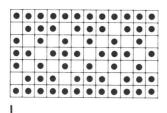

I

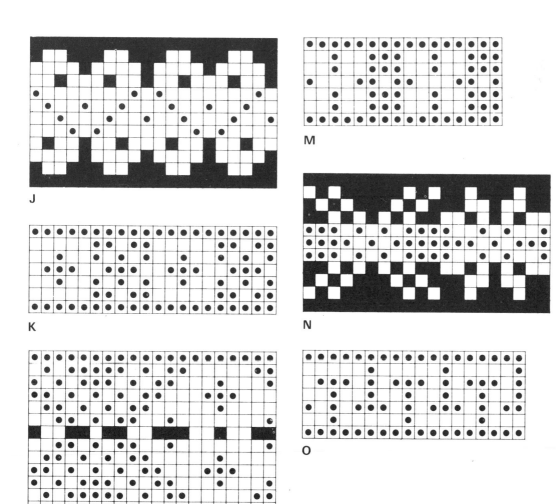

J

K

L

M

N

O

Materials

Shetland 2-ply jumper yarn: 8ozs cream (1a); 7ozs moorit (4), 2ozs black (5).
3 41cm (16in) 3mm (no. 11) double-ended needles.
3 41cm (16in) 2¾mm (no. 12) double-ended needles.
or: 3mm and 2¾mm (nos 11 and 12) circular twin pins, plus a set of 3mm and 2¾mm (nos 11 and 12) double-ended needles.
8 stitch holders.

Tension

9 sts to 2.5cm (1in) on 3mm (no. 11) needles over patterning
9sts to 1in on 2¾mm (no. 12) needles over plain st st.

Instructions

Using 2¾mm (no. 12) needles and base col., cast on 45 sts. Work 2ins plain st st. Change to 3mm (no. 11) needles and work 3ins in Fair Isle patterning. Change to 2¾mm (no. 12) needles and using base col. only, work a further 2ins in plain st st. Cast off.
Your tension square should measure 7ins in length and 5ins across both plain and patterned rows. If your square measures more, use needles a size smaller than quoted, if your square measures less, use needles a size larger.
Using base colour and 2¾mm (no. 12) needles, cast on 145(155:165:175) sts onto 1st needle, cast on 145(155:165:175) sts onto 2nd needle. (290(310:330:350) sts).
With 3rd needle beg working in rounds. (If using twin pin, place markers at end and centre of round to mark side seams.)
Work 7.5(7.5:9:9:10)cms (3:3:3½:3½:4ins) in K2, P2 rib.
Next round: Inc by 10 sts evenly along round, (300(320:340:360) sts).
Change to 3mm (no 11) needles and beg patterning as set in chart in st st (every round K).
Cont until work measures 33(35.5:38:40.5)cms (13:14:15:16ins) from beg. (Check here for length.)

Divide here for front and back
1st round: K12(13:15:16), place on pin.
K126(134:140:148), leave on holder for back.
K12(13:15:16), place on pin. K12(13:15:16), leave on another pin. K126(134:140:148) sts for front. Leave rem 12(13:15:16) sts on pin.
Cont on 126(134:140:148) sts for front.

Front

Work in st st on 2 needles only and in rows, backwards and forwards). Cont without shaping until work measures 14(14:15:16.5)cms (5½:5½:6:6½ins) from beg of armhole. End with a P row.

Neck shaping

K77(84:88:94), leave last 28(34:36:40) sts knitted on holder for centre front neck. K49(50:53:54) to end of row. Cont on last set of stitches for right front.
* Dec 1 st at neck edge only on next 4 rows.
Dec 1 st on neck edge one every other row until 41(42:44:46) sts remain.
Cont without further shaping until work measures 19(19:20.5:21.5)cms (7½:7½:8:8½ins) from beg of armhole.
Leave sts on holder for right shoulder. Rejoin yarn to sts for left front.
Work as for right front from * to end.

Back

Rejoin yarn to 126(134:140:148) sts for back.
Cont in st st on 2 needles only and in rows until work measures 15(15:16.5:18)cms (6:6:6½:7ins) from beg of armhole. End with a P row.

Neck shaping

K77(84:88:94), place last 28(34:36:40) sts knitted on holder for centre back neck. K49(50:52:54) to end.
Cont on these last sts for left back. ** Dec 1 st at neck edge only on next 8 rows. (41(42:44:46) sts).
Cont without further shaping until work measures same as front. Leave sts on holder for left shoulder. Rejoin yarn to sts for right back. Work as for left back from ** to end.

Graft shoulder seams (see p 24)

Neckband

With right side of work facing, using base colour and 2¾mm (no. 12) needles, with 1st needle pick up and K28(29:30:31) sts from left shoulder to sts on holder at centre front neck. 28(32:36:40) sts from holder, 28(29:30:31) sts up to right shoulder.
With 2nd needle pick up and K20(21:22:23) sts down to sts on holder at centre back, 28(32:36:40) sts from holder, 20(21:22:23) sts up to left shoulder.
(152(164:176:188) sts).

Work 10 rounds in K2, P2, rib.
Cast off loosely in rib.

Sleeves
With right side of work facing, use base colour and 2¾mm (no. 12) needles, pick up and K12(13:15:16) sts from left pin, 67(69:72:76) sts to shoulder seam, 67(69:72:76) sts to 2nd pin, 12(13:15:16) sts from pin. (158(164:174:184) sts).
Beg working in rounds. Work 2 rounds st st (every round K).
Change to 3mm (no. 11) needles and beg patterning.

3rd and 4th sizes only:
Next round: K13, sl 1, K2 tog, psso, K to last 16 sts, sl 1, K2 tog, psso, K13 to end.
Next round: K12, sl 1, K2 tog, psso, K to last 15 sts, sl 1, K2 tog, psso, K12 to end.

All sizes
1st round: K11, sl 1, K2 tog, psso, K to last 14 sts, sl 1, K2 tog, psso, K11 to end.
2nd round: K10, sl 1, K2 tog, psso, K to last 13 sts, sl 1, K2 tog, psso, K10 to end.
3rd round: K9, sl 1, K2 tog, psso, K to last 12 sts, sl 1, K2 tog, psso, K9 to end.
4th round: K8, sl 1, K2 tog, psso, K to last 11 sts, sl 1, K2 tog, psso, K8 to end.
5th round: K7, sl 1, K2 tog, psso, K to last 10 sts, sl 1, K2 tog, psso, K7 to end.
6th round: K6, sl 1, K2 tog, psso, K to last 9 sts, sl 1, K2 tog, psso, K6 to end.
7th round: K5, sl 1, K2 tog, psso, K to last 8 sts, sl 1, K2 tog, psso, K5 to end.
8th round: K4, sl 1, K2 tog, psso, K to last 7 sts, sl 1, K2 tog, psso, K4 to end.
9th round: K3, sl 1, K2 tog, psso, K to last 6 sts, sl 1, K2 tog, psso, K3 to end. 122(128:130:140) sts.
Cont to dec 1 st at both ends of every foll 6th round to 88(92:96:100) sts.
Cont without further shaping until work measures 42(44.5:47:51)cms (16½:17½:18½:20ins) from top of shoulder. (Check here for length.)
Change to 2¾mm (no. 12) needles and base colour. Work 2 rounds st st.
Work 5(5:6.5:7.5)cms (2:2:2½:3ins) in K2, P2 rib.
Cast off loosely in rib.

Child's Zip-Neck Jumper

Materials
Shetland 2-ply jumper yarn: 4ozs moorit (1); 2ozs black
(5); 2ozs cream (1a).
3 3¼mm (no. 10) double ended needles.
3 3mm (no. 11) double ended needles.
3 2¾mm (no. 12) double ended needles.
8 stitch holders.
11.5(12.5)cms (4½:5 ins) zip.

Shetland 2-ply jumper yarn
moorit (1), black (5), cream (1a).

Repeats
A 12 sts; B 6 sts; C 18 sts; D 18 sts; E 12 sts; F 4 sts; G 20 sts.

Pattern order
A through to G. 5 plain rows base colour between each band of patterning.

Actual sizes
55(64.5)cms (21½:25½ins) chest.

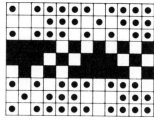

A

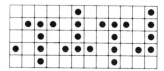

B

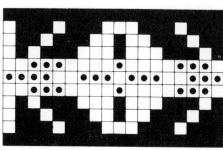

C

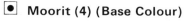

D

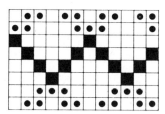

■• Moorit (4) (Base Colour)

■ Black (5)

□ Cream (1a)

E

F

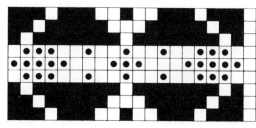

G

60

Tension

8.4 sts to 2.5cms (1in) on $3\frac{1}{4}$mm (no. 10) needles over patterning.

8.4 sts to 2.5cms (1in) on 3mm (no. 11) needles over plain st st.

3mm needles must be used on any plain unpatterned rows/rounds between bands of patterning.

Instructions

Using 3mm (no. 11) needles and base col, cast on 42 sts. Work 2ins in plain st st. Change to $3\frac{1}{4}$mm (no. 10) needles and work 3ins in Fair Isle patterning. Change to 3mm (no. 11) needles and work a further 2ins in base col only and in plain st st. Cast off.

Your tension square should measure 7ins in length and 5ins across both plain and patterned rows. If your square measures more, use needles a size smaller than quoted, if your square measures less, use needles a size larger.

Using base colour and $2\frac{3}{4}$mm (no. 12) needles, cast on 88(106) sts onto 1st needle and 88(106) sts on to 2nd needle. 176(212) sts. Beg knitting in rounds and work 6.5(8)cms ($2\frac{1}{2}$:3ins) in K2, P2 rib. Inc by 4 sts evenly on last round. 180(216) sts. Work 4 rounds st st (every round K) in base colour. Change to $3\frac{1}{4}$mm (no. 10) needles and beg patterning. Work without shaping until work measures 20(24)cms ($8:9\frac{1}{2}$ins) from beg.

Divide for Front and Back

K5(6), place on 1st holder. K85(102), place last 5(6) sts knitted on 2nd holder. K5(6), place on 3rd holder. K80(96), turn. Place rem 5(6) sts on 4th holder.

Front

Cont with 80(96) sts on needle. Work in rows on 2 needles only and in st st (backwards and forwards, turning at each end), without shaping, until work measure 2.5(4)cms ($1:1\frac{1}{2}$ins) from armhole, ending with a wrong side row.

Divide for right and left front

K40(48), cast of 1 st from right-hand needle. Turn. P to end. (39(47) sts.)

* Cont on these sts only for right front until work measures 10(11.5)cms ($4:4\frac{1}{2}$ins) from armhole, ending at armhole edge. Turn. Place first 20(22) sts on holder for

shoulder. Place rem 19(25) sts on another holder for neck ribbing.

Rejoin wool to armhole edge of rem sts for left front. Work to end. 39(47) sts. Work as for right front from * to end.

Back

Rejoin wool to 80(96) sts on middle holder. Work in st st on 2 needles only and without shaping until work measures same as front to end. Leave these sts on the needle.

Graft shoulder seams (see p. 24)

Graft together 20(22) sts from front and back shoulders, beg at armhole edge, for both shoulder seams. Place centre back 40(52) sts on holder.

Neck ribbing

Pick up and K sts in following order:

With right side facing and using 2¾mm (no. 12) needles K19(25) sts of right front beg at neck edge. K40(52) sts across back. K19(25) sts down left front. (78(102) sts.)

Work 4(5)cms (1½:2ins) in K2, P2 rib, beg K2.

Cast off loosely in rib.

Sew in 11(12.5)cms (4½:5 ins) zip.

Sleeves

With right side facing, using base colour and 3mm (no. 11) needles, pick up and K5(6) sts from left holder, 33(37) sts to top of shoulder on to 1st needle. Pick up and K33(37) sts to holder, 5(6) sts from holder on to 2nd needle. (76(86) sts.) Place marker here to indicate end of round.

Using 3rd needle beg working in rounds. Work 2 rounds st st and in base colour. Change to 3¼mm (no. 10) needles and beg patterning.

3rd round: K4, K2 tog, K to last 6 sts, K2 tog, K4 to end.

5th round: K3, K2, tog, K to last 5 sts, K2 tog, K3 to end.

7th round: K2, K2 tog, K to last 4 sts, K2 tog, K2 to end.

8th round: Rep 7th round. (67(78) sts.)

Dec 1 st at both ends of every foll 5th round until 60(68) sts rem.

Cont without further shaping until work measures 23(25.5)cms (9:10ins) from top of shoulder.

Change to 2¾mm (no. 12) needles and, using base colour, work 5(5)cms (2:2ins) in K2, P2 rib.

Cast off loosely in rib.

Fisherman's Jumper

Shetland 2-ply jumper yarn
beige (78), black (5), moorit (4), grey (54).

Repeats
A 6 sts; B 28 sts; C 18 sts.

Pattern order
* A, C, A, B (rep from *).
5 rows base colour between each band of patterning.

Sizes
Actual sizes: 95.5(106.5)cms (37½:42ins).

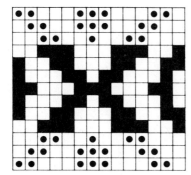

A

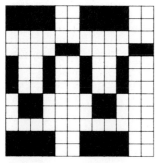

B

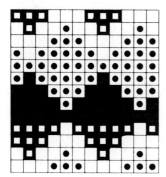

C

■ Black (5)

□ Fawn (78) (Base Colour)

◙ Grey (54)

⊡ Moorit (4)

A pullover using my own choice of colours and traditional Fair Isle patterns such as the tree of life and hearts.

Materials

Shetland 2-ply jumper yarn: 12ozs beige (78); 6ozs black (5); 4ozs moorit (4); 1oz grey (54).
3 3mm and 2¾mm (nos. 11 and 12) 41cm. (16ins) double-ended needles
or: 3mm and 2¾mm (nos. 11 and 12) twin pins plus sets of 3mm and 2¾mm (nos. 11 and 12) double-ended needles.
10 stitch holders.

Tension

9 sts to 2.5cm (1in) or 3mm (no. 11) needles and over patterning.
9 sts to 2.5cm (1in) on 2¾mm (no. 12) needles and over plain st st.
2¾mm (no. 12) needles must be used on any plain unpatterned rows between bands of patterning.

Instructions

Using 2¾mm (no. 12) needles and base col, cast on 45 sts. Work 2ins in plain st st. Change to 3mm (no. 11) needles and work 3ins in Fair Isle patterning. Change to 2¾mm (no. 12) needles and using base col only, work a further 2ins in plain st st. Cast off.
Your tension square should measure 7ins in length and 5ins across both plain and patterned rows. If your square measures more, use needles a size smaller than quoted, if your square measures less, use needles a size larger.
* Using base colour and 2¾mm (no. 12) needles or twin pin, cast on 168(188) sts.
1st row: sl 1, K to end.
Work 1st row 19 times more. **.
Break yarn, leave sts on spare needle.

Front welt

Work as for back welt from * to **.
Work 1 row K2, P2 rib (beg K2). For twin pin, place marker at end of this row to mark side seam. Work across sts on spare needle for back welt in K2, P2 rib (beg K2). For twin pin place 2nd marker at end of this row to mark end of row/round. 336(376) sts. Beg working in rounds. Work 5 rounds in K2, P2 rib as set on previous round. Inc by 0(2) sts evenly along last round. 336(378) sts. Work 6 rounds plain st st (every round K). Change to 3mm (no. 11) needles or twin pin and beg patterning. Cont without further shaping until work measures 33(35.5)cms (13:14ins) from beg.

Top left: *Sample 7, p. 33;*
top right: *Sample 8, p. 34;*
bottom left:
Sample 27, p. 51;
bottom right:
Sample 22, p. 47.

Divide for back and front
next round: K10(12) sts, place on holder. K148(165) sts, K next 20(24) sts and place on holder. K148(165) sts, turn. Place rem 10(12) sts on holder.

Back
Cont on last set of 148(165) sts knitted for back. Work in rows, backwards and forwards, turning at each end. Cont until work measures 25.5(28) cms (11:12ins) from beg of armhole, ending with a P row.
Arrange sts on holder as follows:
K34(40) sts, place on 1st holder for shoulder,
K80(85) sts, place on 2nd holder for back neck,
K34(40) sts, place on 3rd holder for shoulder.

Front
Rejoin yarn to 148(165) sts for front. Work in rows (turning at each end). Cont without further shaping to 8 rows short of finished back length.

Neck shaping
*** Work across 38(44) sts, turn. Cont on these sts only. Dec 1 st at neck edge only on next 4 rows. (34(40) sts). Work 3 more rows. **** Leave these sts on holder for shoulder. Rejoin yarn to arm edge of rem 110(121) sts. Work from *** to ****. Leave centre 72(77) sts on holder for centre front neck.

Graft shoulder seams
With wrong sides of work together, right sides outside, base colour and $2\frac{3}{4}$mm (no. 12) needles, graft right shoulders together using sts still on their needles as shown on p. 24. Beg at arm edge and work until there are 8 sts remaining on each shoulder plus the one final cast off stitch on right hand needle.
Open out the 2 left hand needles, with the right side of the work facing, one needle on the left and the other on the right. Slip the single cast off stitch on to the right hand needle. (17 sts). Cont on these 2 needles only:
1st row: K1 st from left needle, turn.
2nd row: sl 1, P2, turn.
3rd row: sl 1, K3, turn.
4th row: sl 1, P4, turn.
5th row: sl 1, K5, turn.
6th row: sl 1, P6, turn.
7th row: sl 1, K7, turn.
8th row: sl 1, P8, turn.

9th row: sl 1, K9, turn.
10th row: sl 1, P10, turn.
11th row: sl 1, K11, turn.
12th row: sl 1, P12, turn.
13th row: sl 1, K13, turn.
14th row: sl 1, P14, turn.
15th row: sl 1, K15, turn.
16th row: sl 1, P16, turn. 17 sts.
Leave sts on holder.

Neckband
Using base colour and 2¾mm (no. 12) needles and with right side facing, pick up and K sts from around neck as follows:
Beg left of left gusset, pick up and K5(6) sts down left front, 72(77) sts from centre front, 5(6) sts up right front, 17 sts from right gusset, 80(85) sts from centre back and 17 sts from left gusset. (196(208) sts). Place marker here for end of round. Beg working in rounds of K2, P2 rib. Work 2.5 cms (1in). Cast off in rib.

Sleeves
With right side of work facing, using base colour and 2¾mm (no. 12) needles, pick up and K10(12) sts from holder left of side seam, 90(100) sts up to shoulder seam, 90(100) sts down to holder, 10(12) sts rem on holder at base of armhole. (200(224) sts). Place marker here to mark end of round. Work 4 rounds plain st st. Change to 3mm (no. 11) needles and beg patterning, at the same time, work gusset shaping as follows:

2nd size only
5th round: K12, sl 1, K2 tog, psso, K to last 15 sts, sl 1, K2 tog, psso, K12 to end.
6th round: K11, sl 1, K2 tog, psso, K to last 14 sts, sl 1, K2 tog, psso, K11 to end.

All sizes
7th round: K10, sl 1, K2 tog, psso, K to last 13 sts, sl 1, K2 tog, psso, K10 to end.
8th round: K9, sl 1, K2 tog, psso, K to last 12 sts, sl 1, K2 tog, psso, K9 to end.
9th round: K8, sl 1, K2 tog, psso, K to last 11 sts, sl 1, K2 tog, psso, K8 to end.
10th round: K7, sl 1, K2 tog, psso, K to last 10 sts, sl 1, K2 tog, psso, K7 to end.
11th round: K6, sl 1, K2 tog, psso, K to last 9 sts, sl 1, K2

tog, psso, K6 to end.

12th round: K5, sl 1, K2 tog, psso, K to last 8 sts, sl 1, K2 tog, psso, K5 to end.

13th round: K4, sl 1, K2 tog, psso, K to last 7 sts, sl 1, K2 tog, psso, K4 to end.

14th round: K3, sl 1, K2 tog, psso, K to last 6 sts, sl 1, K2 tog, psso, K3 to end.

15th round: K2, sl 1, K2 tog, psso, K to last 5 sts, sl 1, K2 tog, psso, K2 to end.

16th round: K.

17th round: as 15th round.

Rep last 2 round twice more. (152(168) sts).

Dec 1 st at each end of every foll 5th round until 90(100) sts rem. Cont without further shaping until work measures 48.5(53.5)cms (19:21ins) from top of shoulder. Dec by 2(0) sts on last round. (Check here for length.)

Change to 2¾mm (no. 12) needles and work 7.5cms (3ins) in K2, P2 rib.

Cast off loosely in rib.

Man's Round-Neck Jumper

Shetland 2-ply jumper yarn
black (5), moorit (4), cream (1a) – base colour.

Repeats
A 24 sts; B 8 sts; C 19 sts; D 8 sts; E 18 sts. F 6 sts; G 12 sts; H 5 sts; I 24 sts; J 6 sts; K 12 sts; L 8 sts; M 30 sts; N 6 sts; O 16 sts; P 12 sts.

Pattern order
A through to P.
4 plain rows base colour between each band of patterning.

Sizes
Actual size: 102cms (40ins) chest.

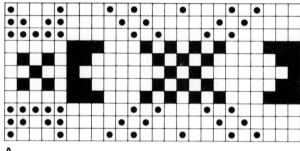

A

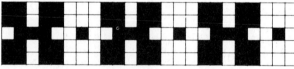

B

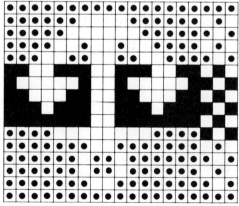

C

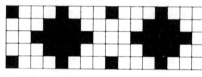

■ Black (5)

⊡ Moorit (4)

☐ Cream (1a) (Base Colour)

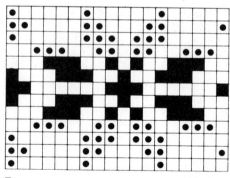

D

E

F

70

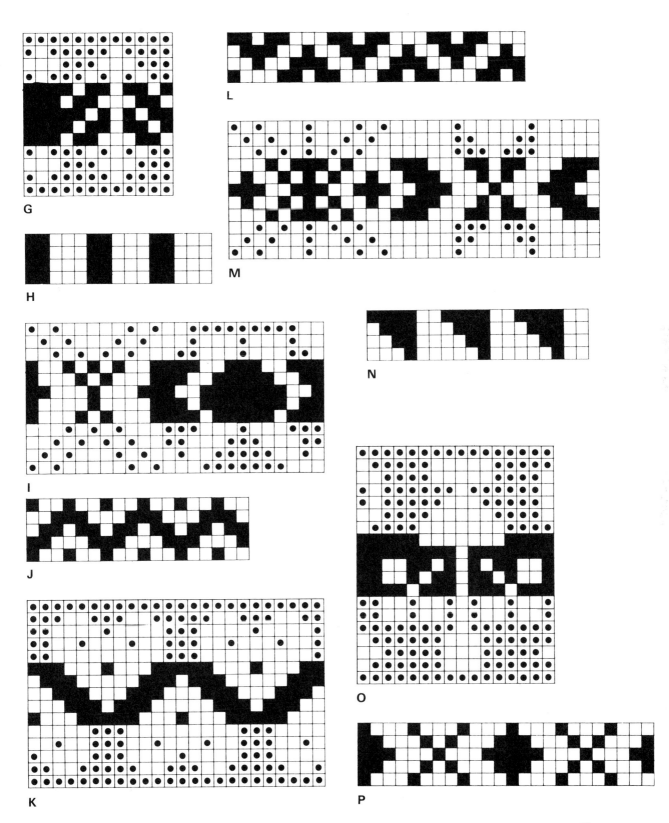

G

H

L

M

N

I

J

O

K

P

71

Materials

Shetland 2-ply jumper yarn: 9ozs cream (1a); 4ozs moorit (4); 4ozs black (5).
3 41cm (16in) 3mm (no. 11) double-ended needles.
3 41cm (16in) 2¾mm (no. 12) double-ended needles.
or: 3mm and 2¾mm (nos 11 and 12) circular twin pins plus a set of 3mm and 2¾mm (nos 11 and 12) double-ended needles.
10 stitch holders or pins.

Tension

9 sts to 2.5cms (1in) on 3mm (no. 11) needles over patterning.
9 sts to 2.5cms (1in) on 2¾mm (no.12) needles over plain st st.

Instructions

Using 2¾mm (no. 12) needles and base col, cast on 45 sts. Work 2in in plain st st. Change to 3mm (no. 11) needles and work 3ins in Fair Isle patterning. Change to 2¾mm (no. 12) needles and using base col only, work a further 2ins in plain st st. Cast off.
Your tension square should measure 7ins in length and 5ins across both plain and patterned rows. If your square measures more, use needles a size smaller than quoted, if your square measures less, use needles a size larger. With base colour and 2¾mm (no. 12) needles or twin pin, cast on 180 sts on to 1st needle. (If using twin pin, place marker here for side seam.) Cast on 180 sts on to 2nd needle (place marker here for end of round on twin pin). (360 sts).

Work 1 round K3, P3 rib.
Join black yarn and work in rib as follows:
* K3 cream, P3 black, rep from * to end.
Work 12 rounds (carry spare yarn behind work).
Work 12 rounds K3 cream, P3 moorit.
Work 12 rounds K3 cream, P3 black.
Work 6 rounds in st st in base colour.
Change to 3mm (no. 11) needles or twin pin and beg patterning as set in chart.
Cont without shaping until work measures 38cm (15ins) from beg. (Check here for length).

Divide for front and back

1st round: K15, place on 1st pin for armhole, K165, place last 15 sts knitted on 2nd pin, K15, place on 3rd pin. K150, turn. Place remaining 15 sts on 4th pin. Cont on the last set of 150 sts for front.

Front: Continue on 2 needles only (if using twin pin, turn at end of each row) and in st st, in rows, turning at each end, until work measures 13cms (5ins) from beg of armhole. End with a P row.

Next row: K98, place last 46 sts knitted on holder for centre front neck, K52 to end.

Cont on these sts only for right front.

** Dec 1 st at neck edge only on next 4 rows (48 sts).

Dec 1 st at neck edge only on next 3 alt rows (45 sts).

Dec 1 st at neck edge only on every following 3rd row to 42 sts.

Cont without further shaping until work measures 23cms (9ins) from armhole. Leave sts on holder for shoulder.

Return to 52 sts for left front and rep instructions for right front from ** to end.

Back: Rejoin wool to 150 sts for back. Work in rows without shaping until work measures 19cms (7½ins) from armhole, ending with a P row.

K103, place last 56 sts knitted on holder for centre back neck, K47 to end.

Cont on these sts only for left back.

*** Dec 1 st at neck edge only on next 3 rows (44 sts).

Dec 1 st at neck edge only on next 2 alt rows (42 sts).

Cont straight until work measures same as front to the shoulder.

Place sts on holder for shoulder.

Rejoin wool to 47 sts for right back, work as for left back from *** to end.

Graft shoulder seams (see p. 24)

Neck ribbing

With right side facing, using base colour and 2¾mm (no. 12) needles, rejoin yarn at right shoulder seam.

Pick up and K16 sts to centre back neck, 56 sts from holder, 16 sts up to left shoulder seam, 35 sts down to centre front neck, 46 sts from holder, 35 sts up to right shoulder seam, (204 sts).

Beg working in rounds. Work 1 round K3, P3 rib in base colour only.

Join black yarn and work 10 rounds as follows:

*K3 cream, P3 black, rep from * to end.

Work 1 round K3, P3 rib in base colour only.

Cast off in rib.

Sleeves

With right side of work facing, using base colour and $2\frac{3}{4}$mm (no. 12) needles, pick up and K15 sts from left pin, pick up and K78 sts to shoulder, 78 sts down to sts on rem pin, K15 sts from pin. Place marker here for end of round (186 sts).

K2 rounds base colour, change to 3mm (no. 11) needles and beg patterning, (186 sts).

1st round: K14, sl 1, K2 tog, psso, K to last 17 sts, sl 1, k2 tog, psso, K14 to end.

2nd round: K13, sl 1, K2 tog, psso, K to last 16 sts, sl 1, K2 tog, psso, K13 to end.

3rd round: K12, sl 1, K2 tog, psso, K to last 15 sts, sl 1, K2 tog, psso, K12 to end.

4th round: K11, sl 1, K2 tog, psso, K to last 14 sts, sl 1, K2 tog, psso, K11 to end.

5th round: K10, sl 1, K2 tog, psso, K to last 13 sts, sl 1, K2 tog, psso, K10 to end.

6th round: K9, sl 1, K2 tog, psso, K to last 12 sts, sl 1, K2 tog, psso, K9 to end.

7th round: K8, sl 1, K2 tog, psso, K to last 11 sts, sl 1, K2 tog, psso, K8 to end.

8th round: K7, sl 1, K2 tog, psso, K to last 10 sts, sl 1, K2 tog, psso, K7 to end.

9th round: K6, sl 1, K2 tog, psso, K to last 9 sts, sl 1, K2 tog, psso, K6 to end.

10th round: K5, sl 1, K2 tog, psso, K to last 8 sts, sl 1, K2 tog, psso, K5 to end.

11th round: K4, sl 1, K2 tog, psso, K to last 7 sts, sl 1, K2 tog, psso, K4 to end.

12th round: K3, sl 1, K2 tog, psso, K to last 6 sts, sl 1, K2 tog, psso, K3 to end.

13th round: K.

14th round: Rep 12th round. (134 sts).

Dec 1 st at both ends of every following 7th round until 90 sts remain.

Continue without further shaping until work measures 46cms (18ins) from shoulder. (Check here for length.)

Change to $2\frac{3}{4}$mm (no. 12) needles and work 4 rounds in base colour.

Work 4 rounds in K3, P3 rib.

Join black yarn and work 8 rounds K3 cream P3 black rib.

Work 8 rounds in K3 cream, P3 moorit.

Work a further 8 rounds K3 cream, P3 black rib.

Work 1 round in rib in base colour only.

Cast off in rib.

Man's Round-Neck Pullover

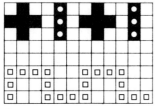

A

B

- ◨ Red (55)
- ▲ Green (30)
- ☐ Grey (2)
- ▢ Purple (19)
- ■ Blue (21)

C

D

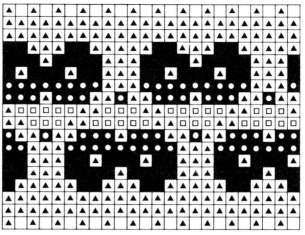

E

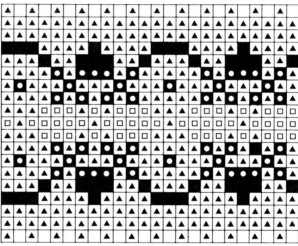

F

Shetland 2-ply jumper yarn
red (55), green (30), grey (2), purple (19), blue (21).

Repeats
A 6 sts; B 6 sts; C 22 sts; D 10 sts; E 12 sts; F 12 sts.

Pattern order
A, C, B, D, A, E, B, F, A.
2 rows plain base colour between each band of patterning.

Sizes
Actual size: 93(96.5:102:107)cms (36½:38:40:42ins) chest.

Materials

Shetland 2-ply jumper yarn: 3:4:4:4ozs grey (2); 3:4:4:5ozs green (30); 1:1:1:1oz purple (19); 1:1:1:1oz blue (21); 1:1:2:2ozs red (55).

3 41cm (16in) 3mm (no. 11) double-ended needles.

3 41cm (16in) 2¾mm (no. 12) double-ended needles.

or: 3mm and 2¾mm (nos 11 and 12) circular twin pin, plus a set of 2¾mm (no. 12) double-ended needles.

8 stitch holders or pins.

Tension

9 sts to 2.5cms (1in) on 3mm (no. 11) needles over patterning.

9 sts to 2.5cms (1in) on 2¾mm (no. 12) needles over plain st st.

Note: Repeats

On pattern C, for sizes 96.5:102:107cms (38:40:42ins) chest use only 2 sts in the space either side of the black triangles (green), instead of 3 sts as shown in the chart. (Repeat will then be over 20 sts instead of 22 sts).

Instructions

Using 2¾mm (no. 12) needles and base col, cast on 45 sts. Work 2ins in plain st st. Change to 3mm (no. 11) needles and work 3ins in Fair Isle patterning. Change to 2¾mm (no. 12) needles and using base col only, work a further 2ins in plain st st. Cast off.

Your tension square should measure 7ins in length and 5ins across both plain and patterned rows. If your square measures more, use needles a size smaller than quoted, if your square measures less, use needles a size larger.

With base colour and 2¾mm (no. 12) needles or twin pin, cast on 165(171:180:190) sts onto 1st needle or twin pin (place marker here for side seam). Cast on 165(171:180:190) sts onto 2nd needle or twin pin (for twin pin only, place marker here for end of round). (330:342:360:380 sts). With 3rd needle or twin pin beg working in rounds.

Work 1 round K3, P3 rib.

Join green yarn and work 6.5(6.5:7.5:7.5)cms (2½:2½:3:3ins) rib as follows: *K3 grey, P3 green, rep from * (carry spare yarn behind work).

2nd size only: dec by 2 sts on last round.

All sizes: Break green yarn, work 3 rounds in st st and base colour only. Change to 3mm (no. 11) needles and beg patterning as set in chart. Cont without shaping until work measures 35.5(37:39.5:41)cms (14:14½:15½:16ins) from beg. (Check here for length.)

Divide for front and back

K157(161:170:179), cast off the following 16(18:20:22) sts,

K149(152:160:168), cast off the following 16(18:20:22) sts,

K149(152:160:168), turn. Cont on these sts only for front, working in *rows*, turning at each end, working backwards and forwards.

Front

Dec 1 st at both ends of next 4 rows.

Dec 1 st at both ends of the next 3 alt rows.

Dec 1 st at both ends of every foll 3rd row to 129(132:140:148) sts.

Work without further shaping until armhole measures 7(7:7.5:7.5)cms (2¾:2¾:3:3ins) ending with a P row.

Divide for right and left fronts

Next row: K77(79:84:90), place last 25(26:28:32) sts knitted on holder for centre front neck, K52(53:56:58) to end of row.

Cont on these sts only for right front.

*Dec 1 st at neck edge only on next 6 rows.

Dec 1 st at neck edge only on next 5 alt rows. (41:42:45:47 sts).

Cont without further shaping until work measures 24(25.5:27:29)cms (9½:10:10½:11ins) from beg of armhole, leave sts on holder.

Rejoin yarn to 52(53:56:58) sts for left front, work as for right front from * to end.

Back

Rejoin yarn to 149(152:160:168) sts for back, work in rows.

Dec 1 st at both ends of next 4 rows.

Dec 1 st at both ends of next 3 alt rows.

Dec 1 st at both ends of every foll 3rd row to 129(132:140:148) sts.

Cont without further shaping until work measures same as front to end, ending with a P row.

Next row: K41(42:45:47), place on holder for shoulder, K47(48:50:54), place on holder for back neck, K41(42:45:47), place on holder for shoulder.

Graft shoulder seams (see p. 24)

Neck ribbing
With right side of work facing, using base colour and
2¾mm (no. 12) needles, pick up and K sts in foll order:
K47(48:50:54) sts from pin at back neck, K63(68:72:74)
sts down to centre front neck, K25(26:28:32) sts from
front pin, K63(68:72:74) sts up to shoulder.
(198:210:222:234 sts).
Work 1 round in K3, P3 rib.
Join green yarn and work 2.5cms (1in) in K3 grey, P3
green.
Cast off in rib.

Armhole ribbing
With right side of work facing, using base colour and
2¾mm (no. 12) needles, pick up and K90(93:96:99) sts
from centre of base of armhole to top of shoulder,
90(93:96:99) sts down to centre of base of armhole.
(180:186:192:198 sts).
Work 1 round K3, P3 rib.
Join green yarn and work 2.5cms (1in) in K3 grey, P3
green rib.
Cast off in rib.

*Man's cross neck jumper
using traditional colours
and designs taken from a
jumper found on Fair Isle.*

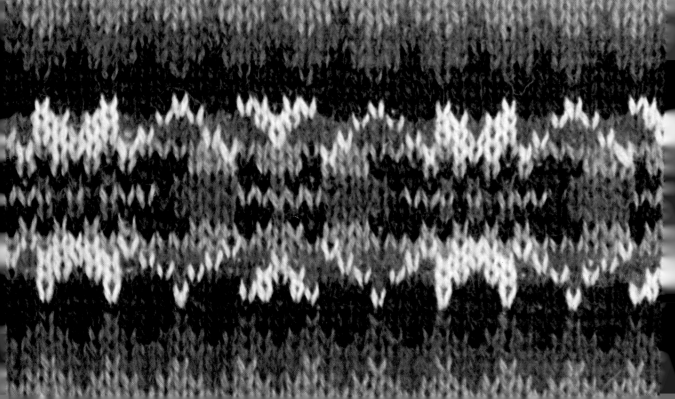

Lady's Yoked Cardigan

top left and right:
*Children's sleeveless
pullover and cardigan in
traditional patterns and
colours.*
bottom: *Sample 28, p. 52.*

Shetland 2-ply jumper yarn

beige (78), cream (1a), purple (19), dark purple (FC10),
pink (72), red (55).

Repeats
A 30 sts; B 19 sts.

Sizes
Actual sizes: 91(96.5:101.5)cms, (36:38:40ins).

☐ Purple (19)

■ Dark Purple (FC10)

☐ Cream (1a)

● Pink (72)

◨ Red (55)

▪ Fawn (78)

v = K2 tog.

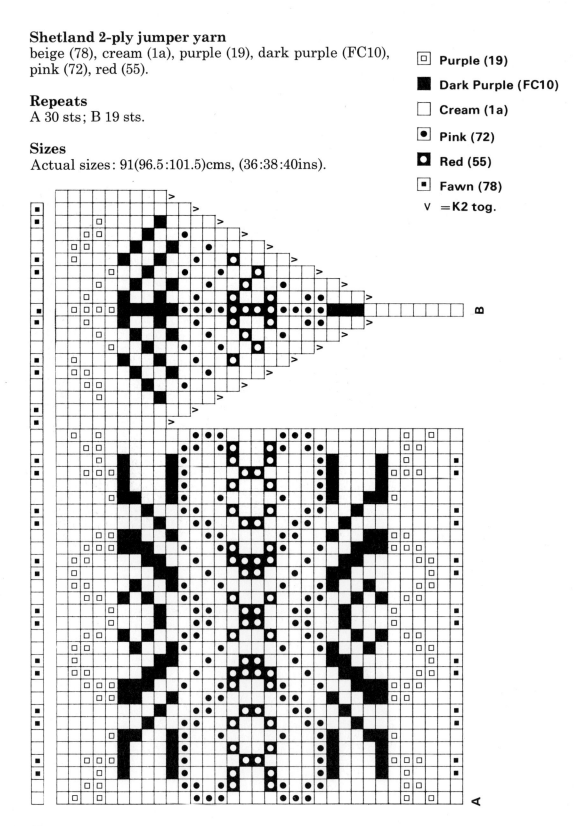

82

Materials

Shetland 2-ply jumper yarn: 10:10:12ozs beige (78); 2ozs cream (1a); approx ½oz oddments in each of the following contrast colours: purple (19), dark purple (FC10), pink (72), red (55).

Set of 3¼mm (no. 10) double-ended 41cms (16in) needles.

Set of 2¾mm (no. 12) double-ended 41cms (16in) needles.

or: 3¼mm and 2¾mm (nos 10 and 12) twin pins and a set of 3¼mm and 2¾mm (nos 10 and 12) double-ended needles.

9 stitch holders.

Buttons.

Tension

8.4 sts to 2.5cms (1in) on 3¼mm (no. 10) needles over patterning.

7.5 sts to 2.5cms (1in) on 3¼mm (no. 10) needles over plain st st.

Instructions

Using no. 10 needles and base col, cast on 38 sts. Work 5ins in plain st st. Cast off. Your square should measure 5ins across and 5ins in length.

Using no. 10 needles and base col, cast on 42 sts. Work 5ins in Fair Isle patterning. Cast off. Your square should measure 5ins across and 5ins in length. If your squares measure more, use needles a size smaller than quoted, if your squares measure less, use needles a size larger.

Using 2¾mm (no. 12) needles or twin pin and base colour cast on 60(64:68) sts. Place marker here for side seam. Cast on a further 126(132:138) sts, place 2nd marker here for other seam. Cast on 60(64:68) sts. 246(260:274) sts. Beg working in *rows*, turning at each end. Work 10cms (4ins) in K1, P1 rib.

Change to 3¼mm (no. 10) needles or twin pin and beg working in st st. Inc 1 st at either side of both markers (thereby increasing by 4 sts in 1 row) on every 10th row to 262(276:290) sts. Cont without further shaping until work measures 38cms (15ins) from beg, ending with a P row. Check here for length.

Divide for front and back

K58(61:64) sts. Cast off foll 12(14:16) sts. K192(201:210) sts to end.

Next row: P58(61:64) sts. Cast off foll 12(14:16) sts. P122(126:130). Turn. Cont on these sts for back.

Back

Dec 1 st at both ends of every foll K row to 110(112:114) sts, ending with a P row.

Next row: K39(40:41). Turn. Cont on these sts only for right back.
* Dec 1 st at both ends of every K row until 1 st remains. Cast off. Rejoin wool to armhole edge of rem sts, work across 39(40:41) sts. Turn. Cont on these sts only for left back. Place rem 32 sts on holder for centre back yoke. Work as for right back from * to end.

Front
** Rejoin wool to right front at armhole edge of 58(61:64) sts.
Dec 1 st at armhole edge only on every K row to 51(54:56) sts.
End at front edge.
K16. Place on holder for centre front yoke.
Dec 1 st at both ends of every K row until 1 st remains. Cast off.
Repeat for left front from **.

Sleeves
With base colour and set of $2\frac{3}{4}$mm (no. 12) double-ended needles, cast on 72 sts. Place marker at end of round. Work 6.5cms ($2\frac{1}{2}$ins) in rounds of K1, P1 rib.
Change to $3\frac{1}{4}$mm (no. 10) needles and work in st st (every round K).
Inc 1 st at each end of every 8th round to 104(106:110) sts.
Cont without further shaping until work measures 44.5(47:51)cms ($17\frac{1}{2}$:$18\frac{1}{2}$:20ins) from beg. Check here for length.
Next round: K99(100:104). Cast off the foll 10(12:12) sts. Cont in st st but *in rows*, turning at each end. Dec 1 st at each end of every K row to 42 sts. Leave on holder for yoke.

Yoke
Join raglan seams.
With right side facing, using base colour and $3\frac{1}{4}$mm (no. 10) needles or twin pin, pick up and K16 sts from holder on right front. Pick up and K35 sts to top of sleeve, 42 sts from holder across top of sleeve, 37 sts down to sts at centre back, 32 sts from holder, 37 sts up to sleeve, 42 sts from holder across top of sleeve, 35 sts down left front to sts on holder, 16 sts from holder. 292 sts.
1st row: P.
2nd row: K.
3rd row: Work 1st row of charts A and B. Beg with last 14 sts of chart A, end with first 14 sts of chart A.

84

Beg decreases on 10th row of chart on this and every foll K row until 184 sts rem as follows:

Dec 1 st (K2 tog tbl), using the 2 sts before and after the 30 sts of chart A. Work to last row of chart. Work 8 sts of chart. * K2 tog tbl, K1, rep from * but keep colours in correct order.

Work to last 8 sts. Work without further shaping to end of row (128 sts).

Next row: P (base colour only).

Next row: K9 ** K2 tog, K3. Rep from ** to last 9 sts, K9 to end. (106 sts).

Next row: P.

Change to 2¾mm (no. 12) needles or twin pin and work 2ins in K1, P1 rib.

Cast off loosely in rib, fold to inside and loosely catch down.

Button bands

With base colour and 2¾mm (no. 12) needles or twin pin, cast on 13 sts.

Work the appropriate length in K1, P1 rib.

Cast off in rib.

With base colour and 2¾mm (no. 12) needles or twin pin cast on 13 sts.

Work the same length as button band, but make buttonholes 5 sts wide at 7.5cm (3ins) intervals.

Pin and sew bands to front opening of cardigan.

Child's Hat and Scarf

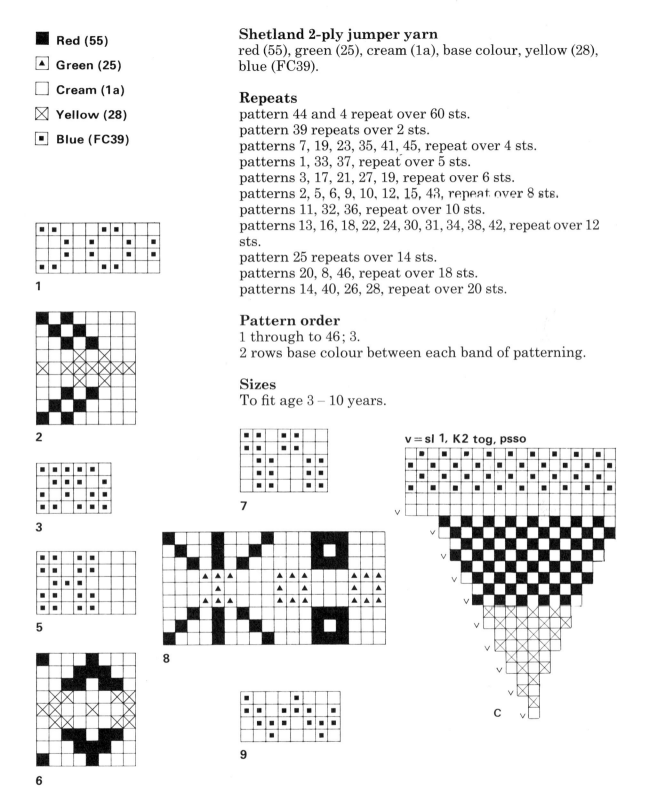

Key

■ Red (55)

▲ Green (25)

☐ Cream (1a)

☒ Yellow (28)

▪ Blue (FC39)

Shetland 2-ply jumper yarn

red (55), green (25), cream (1a), base colour, yellow (28), blue (FC39).

Repeats

pattern 44 and 4 repeat over 60 sts.

pattern 39 repeats over 2 sts.

patterns 7, 19, 23, 35, 41, 45, repeat over 4 sts.

patterns 1, 33, 37, repeat over 5 sts.

patterns 3, 17, 21, 27, 19, repeat over 6 sts.

patterns 2, 5, 6, 9, 10, 12, 15, 43, repeat over 8 sts.

patterns 11, 32, 36, repeat over 10 sts.

patterns 13, 16, 18, 22, 24, 30, 31, 34, 38, 42, repeat over 12 sts.

pattern 25 repeats over 14 sts.

patterns 20, 8, 46, repeat over 18 sts.

patterns 14, 40, 26, 28, repeat over 20 sts.

Pattern order

1 through to 46; 3.

2 rows base colour between each band of patterning.

Sizes

To fit age 3 – 10 years.

v = sl 1, K2 tog, psso

1

2

3

5

6

7

8

9

C

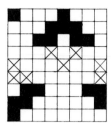

10

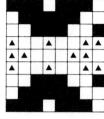

12

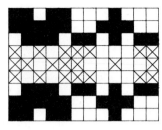

18

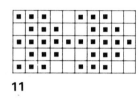

11

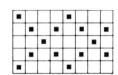

13

19

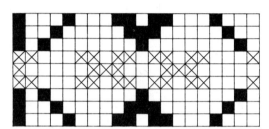

14

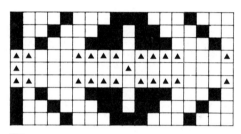

20

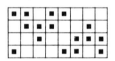

15

21

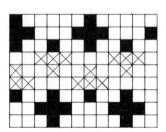

16

22

17

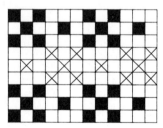

23

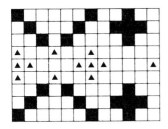

24

25

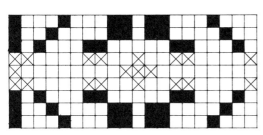

26

27

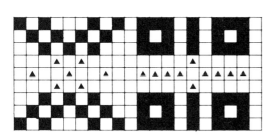

28

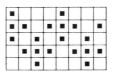

29

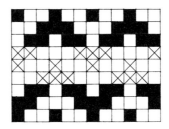

30

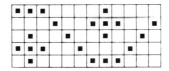

31

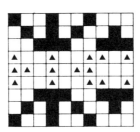

32

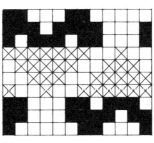

33

34

35

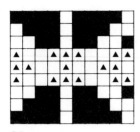

36

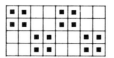

41

37

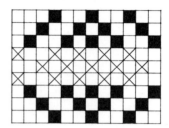

42

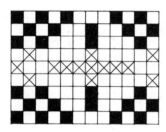

38

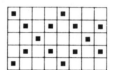

43

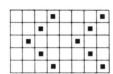

45

39

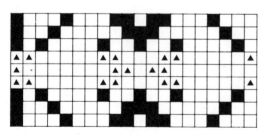

40

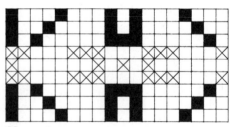

46

Materials
Shetland 2-ply jumper yarn: 2ozs blue (FC39); 2ozs green (25); 2ozs yellow (28); 4ozs red (55); 6ozs cream (1a).
3 3mm (no. 11) double-ended needles.
3 3¼mm (no. 10) double-ended needles.

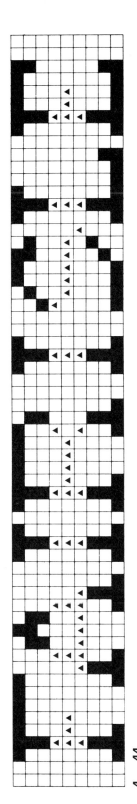

Tension

8.4 sts to 2.5cms (1in) on 3¼mm (no. 10) needles over patterning.

8.13 sts to 2.5cms (1in) on 3mm (no. 11) needles over plain st st.

Instructions

Using 3mm (no. 11) needles and base col, cast on 42 sts. Work 2ins in plains st. st. Change to 3¼mm (no. 10) needles and work 3ins in Fair Isle patterning. Change to 3mm (no. 11) needles and work a further 2ins in base col only and in plain st st. Cast off.

Your tension square should measure 7ins in length and 5ins across both plain and patterned rows. If your square measures more, use needles a size smaller than quoted; if your square measures less, use needles a size larger.

Hat

Using base colour and 3mm (no. 11) needles cast on 72 sts on 1st needle, 72 sts on to 2nd needle. (144 sts). With 3rd needle beg working in rounds in K2, P2 rib for 13cm (5ins).

Change to 3¼mm (no. 10) needles and work 4 rounds st st (every row K) in base colour, then beg patterning with pattern 39, then 38, then 39.

In base col only: 1st round K, 2nd round, * K11, K2 tog. Rep from * to end of round (133 sts). Begin pattern C for crown.

Pull yarn through last sts to wrong side, secure and weave in end.

Scarf

Using base colour and 3mm (no. 11) needles cast on 60 sts on 1st needle and 60 sts on 2nd needle. (120 sts). With 3rd needle beg working in rounds in K2, P2 rib for 6 rounds.

Change to 3¼mm (no. 10) needles and work 4 rounds st st in base colour. Beg patterning.

Work until scarf measures 119.5cm (47ins) from beg. End with 4 rounds of base colour.

Change to 3mm (no. 11) needles and work 6 rounds in K2, P2 rib.

Cast off loosely in rib.

Make tassels to required length.

Make sure the end of each round (side seam) is in line. Join tassels to ends of scarf, sewing both sides together at ribbing.

Child's Cardigan

Shetland 2-ply jumper yarn
moorit (4), yellow (46), beige (3), pink (101), cream (1a), blue (FC39).

Repeats
A 12 sts; B 4 sts.

Pattern order
B, * A, B. (rep from *).
1 row base colour between each band of patterning.

Sizes
Actual size: 63:5(67.5:73.5)cms (25:26½:29ins).

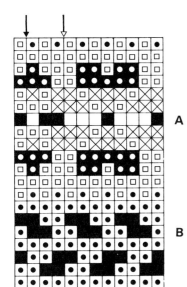

A

B

☐ **Cream (1a)**

■ **Brown (4)**

⊠ **Yellow (46)**

▣ **Blue (FC39)**

◨ **Pink (101)**

⊡ **Beige (3)**

↓ **1st and 2nd sizes only, beg. each round here**

↓ **3rd size only, beg. each round here**

Materials
Shetland 2-ply jumper yarn: 2:3:3ozs blue (FC39); 1:2:2ozs pink (101); 1:2:2ozs yellow (46); 4:4:6ozs beige (3); 1:1:1oz cream (1a); 1:2:2ozs moorit (4).
3 3mm (no. 11) double-ended needles.
3 2¾mm (no. 12) double-ended needles.
or: 3mm and 2¾mm (nos 11 and 12) circular twin pins and 3 3mm and 2¾mm (nos 11 and 12) double-ended needles.
8 stitch holders.
6 buttons.

Tension
9 sts to 2.5cms (1in) on 3mm (no. 11) needles and over patterning.
9 sts to 2.5cms (1in) on 2¾mm (no. 12) needles and over plain st st.
2¾mm (no. 12) needles must be used on any plain unpatterned rows/rounds between bands of patterning.

Instructions

Using 2¾mm (no. 12) needles and base col, cast on 45 sts. Work 2ins in plain st st. Change to 3mm (no. 11) needles and work 3ins in Fair Isle patterning. Change to 2¾mm (no. 12) needles and using base col only, work a further 2ins in plain st st. Cast off.

Your tension square should measure 7ins in length and 5 ins across both plain and patterned rows. If your square measures more, use needles a size smaller than quoted, if your square measures less, use needles a size larger.

Using 2¾mm (no. 12) needles or twin pin and base colour, cast on 55(58:63) sts onto 1st needle. (If using twin pin, mark last st with coloured thread to mark side seam). Cast on 110(116:126) sts onto 2nd needle. (If using twin pin mark last st with coloured thread for 2nd side seam). Cast on 55(58:63) sts onto 3rd needle. (220(232:252) sts). Beg working in rounds (knitting sts from 1st needle onto 3rd needle), *but* before beginning each round wrap yarn 10 times round right-hand needle for the front opening. (For twin pin, work in rows, turning at each end of row/round.)

Work 4(5:5)cms (1½:2:2ins) in K2, P2 rib.

Next round: Cont in rib but increase by 2 sts on left front, 4 sts on back and 2 sts on right front evenly along round. (228(240:260) sts).

Work 4 rows st st (every row K) in base colour, then beg patterning and change to 3mm (no. 11).

Cont without shaping until work measures 25.5(28:30.5)cms (10:11:12ins). from beginning. (Check here for length.)

Divide for front and back

Next round: K57(60:65), leave last 10(11:12) sts knitted on 1st holder. K10(11:12), leave on 2nd holder, K104(109:118), leave last 10(11:12) sts knitted on 3rd holder. (K10(11:12), leave on 4th holder. K47(49:53) to end.

Front

Wrap yarn 10 times round right-hand needle, then K next 47(49:53) sts of left front. (For twin pin K left and right fronts separately.)

Cont working on these 2 sets of sts for left and right fronts and cont to wrap yarn around needle at centre for front opening.

Work in st st on 2 needles only and in rows, backwards and forwards, turning at each end. (If using twin pin,

turn at the end of each row.)
Cont without shaping until work measures
9(10:11.5)cms ($3\frac{1}{2}$:4:$4\frac{1}{2}$ins) from armhole, ending with a
P row.

Neck shaping
1st row: K47(48:53), turn. Cont on these sts only for
right front.
2nd row: Cast off 11(11:12) sts. P to end.
* Dec 1 st at neck edge only on next 8(10:10) rows.
(24(28:30) sts).
Cont without shaping until work measures
$12\frac{1}{2}$(14:15.5)cms (5:$5\frac{1}{2}$:6ins) from beg of armhole. Leave
sts on holder for right shoulder.
Return to 47(49:53) sts on needle for left front. Rejoin
yarn at neck edge. Cast off 11(11:12) sts. K to end of row.
Work as from * to end.

Back
Return to 94(96:106) sts. Work on 2 needles only in st st
(if using twin pin, turn at end of each row) until work
measures 10(11.5:13) cms (4:$4\frac{1}{2}$:5ins) from beginning of
armhole, ending with a P row.

Neck shaping
K63(66:71). leave last 32(34:36) sts knitted on holder. K
to end. 31(32:35) sts.
Cont on these sts for right back.
** Dec 1 st at neck edge only on next 7(4:5) rows.
(24(28:30) sts).
Cont without shaping until work measures same as
front.
Leave these sts on holder for shoulder.
Return to 31(32:35) sts and work as from ** to end.

Graft shoulder seams (see p. 24)

Sleeves
With right side of work facing and using $2\frac{3}{4}$mm (no. 12)
needles and base colour, K10(11:12) sts from 2nd holder,
pick up and K45(50:54) sts along armhole on to 1st needle
to top of shoulder. K45(50:54) sts down to 1st holder.
K10(11:12) sts from holder on to 2nd needle.
(110(122:132) sts). (If using twin pin mark last st with
coloured thread to mark end of round.)
Work 2 rows in base colour. Change to 3mm (no. 11)
needles and beg patterning.
3rd round: K10(11:12), K2 tog, K to last 12(13:14) sts,

K2 tog, K10(11:12) to end.

4th round: K9(10:11), K2 tog, K to last 11(12:13) sts, K2 tog, K9(10:11) to end.

5th round: K8(9:10), K2 tog, K to last 10(11:12) sts, K2 tog, K8(9:10) to end.

6th round: K7 (8:9), K2 tog, K to last 9(10:11) sts, K2 tog, K7(8:9) to end.

7th round: K6(7:8), K2 tog, K to last 8(9:10) sts, K2 tog, K6(7:8) to end.

8th round: K5(6:7), K2 tog, K to last 7(8:9) sts, K2 tog, K5(6:7) to end.

9th round: K4(5:6), K2 tog, K to last 6(7:8) sts, K2 tog, K4(5:6) to end.

10th round: K3(4:5), K2 tog, K to last 5(6:7) sts, K2 tog, K3(4:5) to end.

11th round: K2(3:4), K2 tog, K to last 4(5:6) sts, K2 tog, K2(3:4) to end.

2nd and 3rd sizes only

12th round: K2(3), K2 tog, K to last 4(5) sts, K2 tog, K2(3) to end.

3rd size only

13th round: K2, K2 tog, K to last 4 sts, K2 tog, K2 to end.

All sizes

Dec 1 st at both ends of every 5th round until 64(72:80) sts remain.

Cont without shaping until work measures 27(29:32)cms (10$\frac{1}{2}$:11$\frac{1}{2}$: 12$\frac{1}{2}$ins) from top of shoulder. (Check here for length.)

Change to 2$\frac{3}{4}$mm (no. 12) needles and work 4(5:6.5) cms (1$\frac{1}{2}$:2:2$\frac{1}{2}$ins) in K2, P2 rib.

Cast off loosely in rib.

Work 2nd sleeve as 1st, but using sts from 4th and 3rd pins.

Neckband

With right side of work facing, using base colour and 2$\frac{3}{4}$mm (no. 12) needles or twin pin, pick up and K23(23:24) sts from front neck, 16(16:17) sts up to shoulder, 6(7:8) sts down to sts on holder at back neck, 32(34:36) sts from holder, 6(7:8) sts up to shoulder, 16(16:17) sts down to centre front neck, 23(23:24) sts from front. (122(126:134) sts).

Work 2.5cms (1in) in K2, P2 rib.

Cast off in rib.

Button band

Cut and tie yarn at front opening (see p. 20).

With right side of work facing, and using 2 $2\frac{3}{4}$mm (no. 12) needles or twin pin, pick up and K140(156:170) sts along front edge. Work 2.5cms (1in) in K2, P2 rib, beg K2.

Cast off loosely in rib.

Buttonhole band

With right side of work facing, using $2\frac{3}{4}$mm (no. 12) needles and base colour, pick up and K140(156:170) sts along front edge.

Work 4 rows in K2, P2 rib.

Next row: Make buttonhole at 5cms (2in) intervals.

Cont in rib until band measures 2.5cms (1in).

Cast off loosely in rib.

Man's Jumper with Cross-Over Collar

Materials

Shetland 2-ply jumper yarn: 6:6:8ozs cream (1a); 7:8:10ozs moorit (4); 2:2:2ozs black (5); 3:3:3ozs yellow (28); 5:6:6ozs red (55); 5:6:6ozs blue (21); 5:6:6ozs green (83).

3 3mm (no. 11) 41cm (16ins) double-ended needles.

3 $2\frac{3}{4}$mm (no. 12) 41cm (16ins) double-ended needles.

or: 3mm and $2\frac{3}{4}$mm (nos 11 and 12) circular twin pins and 3 3mm and $2\frac{3}{4}$mm (nos 11 and 12) double-ended needles.

10 stitch holders.

Tension

9 sts to 2.5 cm (1in) on 3mm (no. 11) needles over patterning.

9 sts to 2.5cm (1in) on $2\frac{3}{4}$mm (no. 12) needles over plain st st.

$2\frac{3}{4}$mm (no. 12) needles must be used for any plain unpatterned rows/rounds between bands of patterning.

Instructions

Using $2\frac{3}{4}$mm (no. 12) needles and base col, cast on 45 sts. Work 2ins in plain st st. Change to 3mm (no. 11) needles and work 3ins in Fair Isle patterning. Change to $2\frac{3}{4}$mm (no. 12) needles and using base col only, work a further 2ins in plain st st. Cast off.

Your tension square should measure 7ins in length and 5ins across both plain and patterned rows. If your square measures more, use needles a size smaller than quoted, if your square measures less, use needles a size larger.

Using base colour and $2\frac{3}{4}$mm (no. 12) needles cast on 156(174:192) sts on 1st needle and 156(174:192) sts on 2nd needle. (312(348:384) sts). With 3rd needle beg working in rounds in K3, P3 rib for 10cm (4ins). (If using twin pin place markers at end and middle of rounds.) Inc by 12sts evenly on last round. (324(360:396) sts).

Work 5 rounds in st st and base colour (every round K). Change to 3mm (no. 11) needles and beg patterning with pattern A and work through chart.

Cont without shaping until work measures 43cm (17ins) from beg. (Check here for length).

Divide for armholes

K13(15:17), place on 1st pin. K136(150:164), place on holder for front. K13(15:17), place on 2nd pin. K13(15:17), place on 3rd pin. K136(150:164). Turn. Place rem 13(15:17) sts on 4th pin.

Cont with 136(150:164) sts on needle for back.

Shetland 2-ply jumper yarn

cream (1a), moorit (4), blue (FC41), green (83), red (55),
yellow (28), black (5).

Repeats

A 36 sts; B 36 sts; C 4 sts; D 18 sts; E 6 sts; F 4 sts; G 6 sts;
H 6 sts; I 6 sts.

Pattern order

* C, A, D, B, E, A, F, B, G, A, H, B, I, A. Rep from *.
5 rows base colour between each band of patterning.

Sizes

Actual size: 91.5:102:112cms (36:40:44ins).

- ⊡ **Moorit (4) (Base Colour)**
- ☐ **Cream (1a)**
- ▪ **Blue (FC41)**
- ⊠ **Yellow (28)**
- ▲ **Green (83)**
- ◉ **Red (55)**
- ■ **Black (5)**

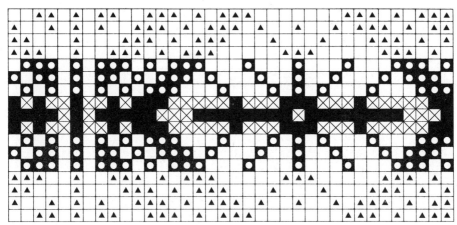

A

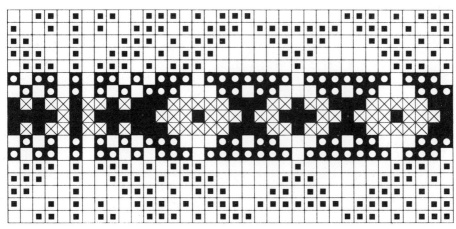

B

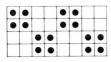

C

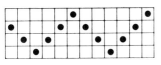

D

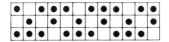

E

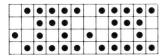

F

G

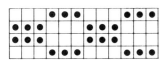

H

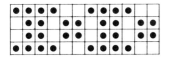

I

Back

Work on 2 needles only (or twin pin) in st st and in rows, turning at each end.

Cont without shaping until armhole measures 16.5(21.5:23)cms (6½:8½:9ins) from beg.

Neck shaping

K89(98:109), place last 42(46:54) sts knitted on holder. K47(52:55) to end.

* Cont on these last sts only, dec 1 st at neck edge only on next 7 rows.

Cont straight until work measures 63.5(68.5:70)cms (25:27:27½ins) from beg. Leave sts on holder. (40(45:48) sts).

Rejoin yarn to 2nd set of 47(52:55) sts. Rep from * to end.

Front

Rejoin yarn to 136(150:164) sts for front, work 8 rows. Divide for neck in the following way:

Work across 50(55:58) sts. Cast off foll 36(40:48) sts, work 50(55:58) sts to end. Cont on these sts only.

** Dec 1 st at neck edge only on every foll 7th row until 40(45:48) sts remain.

Cont without shaping until work measures same as back.

Leave sts on holder for shoulder.

Rejoin yarn to remaining 50(55:58) sts and work as from **.

Graft shoulder seams (see p. 24).

Sleeves

With right side facing, using base colour and 2¾mm (no. 12) needles, pick up and K13(15:17) sts from left pin at armhole, 72(80:88) sts up to shoulder, 72(80:88) sts down to 2nd pin, 13(15:17) sts from pin. 170(190:210) sts.

Place marker here to mark end of round.

Work 2 rounds in base colour and st st. Change to 3mm (no. 11) needles. Beg patterning and shaping:

3rd size only

next round: K17, sl 1, K2 tog, psso, K to last 20 sts, sl 1, K2 tog, psso, K17 to end.

next round: K16, sl 1, K2 tog, psso, K to last 19 sts, sl 1, K2 tog, psso, K16 to end.

2nd and 3rd sizes only

next round: K15, sl 1, K2 tog, psso, K to last 18 sts, sl 1, K2 tog, psso, K15 sts to end.
next round: K14, sl 1, K2 tog, psso, K to last 17 sts, sl 1, K2 tog, psso, K14 to end.
next round: K13, sl 1, K2 tog, psso, K to last 16 sts, sl 1, K2 tog, psso, K13 to end.

All sizes

1st round: K12, sl 1, K2 tog, psso, K to last 15 sts, sl 1, K2 tog, psso, K12 to end.
2nd round: K11, sl 1, K2 tog, psso, K to last 14 sts, sl 1, K2 tog, psso, K11 to end.
3rd round: K10, sl 1, k2 tog, psso, K to last 13 sts, sl 1, K2 tog, psso, K10 to end.
4th round: K9, sl 1, K2 tog, psso, K to last 12 sts, sl 1, K2 tog, psso, K9 to end.
5th round: K8, sl 1, K2 tog, psso, K to last 11 sts, sl 1, K2 tog, psso, K8 to end.
6th round: K7, sl 1, K2 tog, psso, K to last 10 sts, sl 1, K2 tog, psso, K7 to end.
7th round: K6, sl 1, K2 tog, psso, K to last 9 sts, sl 1, K2 tog, psso, K6 to end.
8th round: K5, sl 1, K2 tog, psso, K to last 8 sts, sl 1, K2 tog, psso, K5 to end.
9th round: K4, sl 1, K2 tog, psso, K to last 7 sts, sl 1, K2 tog, psso, K4 to end.
10th round: K3, sl 1, K2 tog, psso, K to last 6 sts, sl 1, K2 tog, psso, K3 to end.
11th round: Rep 10th round. (126(134:146) sts).
Dec 1 st at each end of every foll 6th round to 90(102:114) sts.
Work without further shaping until sleeve measures 39.5(42:44.5)cms (15½:16½:17½ins) from top of shoulder. (Check here for length.)
Change to 2¾mm (no. 12) needles and work 6.5cms (2½ins) in K3, P3 rib.
Cast off in rib.

Collar

With right side of work facing, using base colour and 2¾mm (no. 12) needles of twin pin pick up and K85(93:98) sts up right front side of neck to shoulder, 15 sts down to centre back neck, (42(46:54) sts from holder, 14 sts up to shoulder, 85(93:98) sts down to left front neck. (241:261:279 sts). Cont in K3, P3 rib.

Next row: rib 167(177:186) sts, turn. Sl 1, rib 92, turn, rib to end.

Rib 3 rows.

next row: Rib 158(168:177) sts, turn, sl 1, rib 74, turn, rib to end.

Rib 3 rows.

next row: Rib 149(159:168) sts, turn, sl 1, rib 56, turn, rib to end.

Rib 3 rows.

next row: Rib 140(150:159) sts, turn sl 1, rib 38, turn, rib to end.

Rib 3 rows.

next row: Rib 131(141:150) sts, turn sl 1, rib 21, turn, rib to end.

Cont without further shaping until ribbing measures 11.5cms ($4\frac{1}{2}$ins) from centre back neck to end.

Cast off loosely in rib. Sew side edges of ribbing to cast off edge at centre front.

Man's V-Neck Pullover

Shetland 2-ply jumper yarn

moorit (4), cream (1a), blue (33), rust (FC38), yellow (FC40), grey (2) – base colour.

Repeats

A 8 sts: B 18 sts; C 30 sts.

Pattern order

* A, B, A, C. Rep from *.
4 plain rows base colour between each band of patterning.

Sizes

Actual size: 102 cms (40ins) chest.

- ⊙ Moorit (4)
- ☐ Cream (1a)
- ▪ Blue (33)
- ▫ Rust (FC38)
- ⊠ Yellow (FC40)
- ■ Grey (2) (Base Colour)

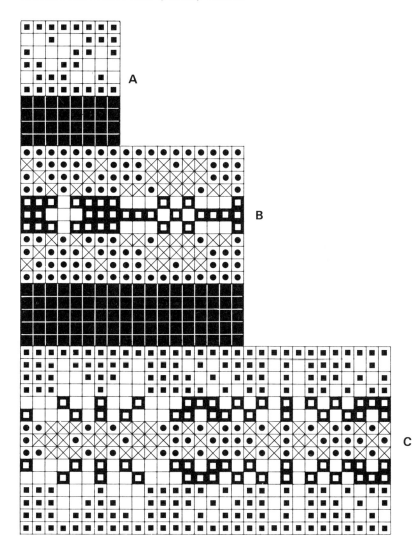

Materials

Shetland 2-ply jumper yarn: 2ozs yellow (FC40); 2ozs blue (33); 2ozs cream (1a); 2ozs rust (FC38); 2ozs moorit (4); 7ozs grey (2).

3 3mm (no. 11) double-ended needles.

3 2¾mm (no. 12) double-ended needles.

or: 3mm and 2¾mm (nos 11 and 12) circular twin pins plus a set of 3mm and 2¾mm (nos 11 and 12) double ended needles.

8 stitch holders.

1 safety pin.

Tension

9 sts to 2.5cms (1in) on 3mm (no. 11) needles and over patterning.

9 sts to 2.5cm and on 2¾mm (no. 12) needles over plain st st.

note 2¾mm (no. 12) needles are to be used for every plain unpatterned row/round between bands of patterning.

Instructions

Using 2¾mm (no. 12) needles and base col, cast on 45 sts. Work 2ins in plain st st. Change to 3mm (no. 11) needles and work 3ins in Fair Isle patterning. Change to 2¾mm (no. 12) needles and using base col only, work a further 2ins in plain st st. Cast off.

Your tension square should measure 7ins in length and 5ins across both plain and patterned rows. If your square measures more, use needles a size smaller than quoted; if your square measures less, use needles a size larger.

With base col and 2¾mm (no. 12) needles or twin pin, cast on 180 sts onto first needle or twin pin (for twin pin mark last st with coloured yarn to mark side seam). Cast on 180 sts onto 2nd needle or twin pin (mark last st with coloured yarn for end of round). 360 sts. With 3rd needle or twin pin beg working in rounds of K2, P2 rib. Work for 10cms (4ins). Work 5 rounds st st (every round K). Change to 3mm (no. 11) needles or twin pin and beg patterning. Cont until work measures 38cms (15ins) from beg.

Divide for front and back

K10 sts and place on holder.

K180 sts and place last 20 sts knitted on holder.

K160 sts, turn (place rem 10 sts on holder).

Back

Cont on last 160 sts knitted for back, on 2 needles only in rows working backwards and forwards, turning at each end. Dec 1 st at each end of next 6 rows (148 sts). Dec 1 st at each end of next 6 alt rows (136 sts). Dec 1 st at each end of foll 3rd row to 134 sts. Cont without further shaping until work measures 27cms (10½ins) from beg of armhole; end with a P row. Leave sts on 3 holders as follows;
K32 sts and leave on holder for right shoulder,
K70 sts and leave on holder for back neck,
K32 sts and leave on holder for left shoulder.

Front

With right side of work facing, join yarn to right edge of 160 sts for front. Working in rows, (1st row K) dec 1 st at each end of next 6 rows. (148 sts).

Right front

K2 tog, K72 sts. Place next st on safety pin, turn. P to end (73 sts). Cont on these sts only, leaving sts not in use on holder.
Work neck edge and armhole edge shaping as follows:
* Dec 1 st at armhole edge only on next 6 alt rows, then on every 3rd row 4 times. *At the same time* dec 1 st at neck edge only on every alt row to 42 sts. Dec 1 st at neck edge only on every foll 3rd row to 32 sts. Cont without further shaping until work measures same as back to end. Leave sts on holder.

Left front

Rejoin yarn to 73 sts on holder for left front at right edge (right side of work facing). Work as for right front from *.
Graft shoulder seams (see p. 24).

Armhole ribbing

Using 2¾mm (no. 12) needles, right side of work facing and base colour, K across 20 sts on holder, pick up and K104 sts to shoulder seam, 104 sts to base of armhole, place marker here to mark end of round. (228 sts). Work 10 rounds in K2, P2 rib. Cast off in rib.

Neck band

With right side of work facing, 2¾mm (no. 12) needles or twin pin and base colour, K across 70 sts on holder at back neck, pick up and K101 sts down right front to pin,

K centre st from pin (leaving pin attached as a marker). Pick up and K101 sts up left front to shoulder. Place marker here to mark end of round. (273 sts). Beg working in rounds of K2, P2 rib: beg P1, ** K2, P2, rep from ** to 2 sts before centre st. P2 tog, K centre st, P2 tog. *** K2, P2, rep from *** to end of round. Cont ribbing as set for 10 rounds *but* cont to dec by P2 tog, either side of centre st, which is to be knitted on every round.
Cast off in rib.

Boy's Round-Neck Pullover

 Green (25)

☐ **Cream (1a)**

◕ **Moorit (4)**

■ **Black (5)**

◻ **Beige (202)**

⊠ **Yellow (66)**

◧ **Apricot (207)**

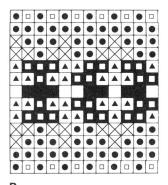

A

B

Shetland 2-ply jumper yarn
moorit (4), yellow (66), black (5), cream (1a), green (25), beige (202), apricot (207).

Repeats
A 12 sts; B 6 sts.

Pattern order

* A, B. (Rep from *).
2 rows of base colour between each band of patterning.

Sizes

Actual size: 67.5:75:77.5cms ($26\frac{1}{2}$:$29\frac{1}{2}$:$30\frac{1}{2}$ins).

Materials

1oz green (25); 1oz yellow (66); 2ozs apricot (207); 2:2:4ozs beige (202); $\frac{1}{2}$oz oddments of: cream (1a) and black (5); 2ozs moorit (4).
3 3mm (no. 11) double-ended needles.
3 $2\frac{3}{4}$mm (no. 12) double-ended needles.
or: 3mm and $2\frac{3}{4}$mm (nos. 11 and 12) circular twin pins, plus a set of $2\frac{3}{4}$mm (no. 12) double-ended needles.
8 stitch holders.

Tension

9 sts to 2.5cms (1in) on 3mm (no. 11) needles over patterning.
9 sts to 2.5cms (1in) on $2\frac{3}{4}$mm (no. 12) needles over plain st st.
Note: $2\frac{3}{4}$mm (no. 12) needles or twin pin must be used on any plain unpatterned rows/rounds between bands of patterning.

Instructions

Using $2\frac{3}{4}$mm (no. 12) needles and base col, cast on 45 sts. Work 2ins in plain st st. Change to 3mm (no. 11) needles and work 3ins in Fair Isle patterning. Change to $2\frac{3}{4}$mm (no. 12) needles and using base col only, work a further 2ins in plains st st. Cast off.
Your tension square should measure 7ins in length and 5ins across both plain and patterned rows. If your square measures more, use needles a size smaller than quoted, if your square measures less, use needles a size larger.
With base col and $2\frac{3}{4}$mm (no. 12) needles cast on 114(126:132) sts onto 2nd needle (if using twin pin mark last st with coloured thread for side seam). Cast on 114(126:132) sts onto 2nd needle (if using twin pin mark last st with different coloured thread for end of round). (228(252:264) sts).
Work 5(6.5:6.5)cms (2:$2\frac{1}{2}$:$2\frac{1}{2}$ins) in K2, P2 rib.
Next row: Increase by 12 sts evenly along round. (240:264:276 sts).
Work 4 rounds in st st (every round) in base col.
Change to 3mm (no. 11) needles, beg patterning and

cont without shaping until work measures
25.5(28:30.5)cms (10:11:12ins) from beg.

Divide for front and back
K7(8:9), place on 1st holder, K106(116:120). K7(8:9),
place on 2nd holder. K7(8:9) place on 3rd holder.
K106(116:120) turn. Place remaining 7(8:9) sts on 4th
holder.

Back
Cont on last 106(116:120) sts knitted for back, on
needles only, in rows, working backwards and forwards
and turning at each end.
Dec 1 st at each end of next 5(6:6) rows. (96:104:108)
sts).
Dec 1 st at each end of every following alternate row
until 86(94:98) sts remain.
Cont without shaping until work measures
10(11.5:13)cms (4:4½:5ins) from beg of armholes.

Neck shaping
K30(33:34). K26(28:30), place on holder. K30(33:34) to
end.
Cont on these last sts only.
* Dec 1 st at neck edge only on next 7(8:8) row. Work
straight until armhole measures 14(15.3:16.5)cms
(5½:6:6½ins). Place sts on holder for shoulder. 23(25:26)
sts. Return to remaining 30(33:34) sts on needle and
work as from * to end.

Front
Rejoin yarn to sts for front. Dec 1 st at both ends of next
5(6:6) rows. (96(104:108) sts). End with a P row.
1st row: K60(65:68), place last 24(26:28) sts knitted on
holder for centre neck, K36(39:40) to end.
Cont on these sts only.
** *2nd row:* Dec 1 st at both ends of row.
3rd row: Dec 1 st at neck edge only.
4th row: Dec 1 st at both ends of row.
Dec 1 st at both ends of next and every foll alt row to
25(28:29) sts.
Dec 1 st at neck edge only on every foll alt row to
23(25:26) sts.
Cont without further shaping until work measures
same as back. Leave sts on holder.
Rejoin yarn to remaining 36(39:40) sts. work as from **
to end.
Graft shoulder seams (see p. 24).

Neck ribbing

With right side of work facing, using base colour and set 2¾mm (no. 12) needles, beg at left shoulder seam, pick up and K55(56:57) sts to holder at centre front,
24(26:28) sts from holder,
55(56:57) sts to right shoulder seam,
24(25:26) sts from right shoulder seam to sts on holder for centre back,
26(28:30) sts from holder,
24(25:26) sts up to left shoulder seam. (208:216:224 sts).
Place marker here to mark end of round.
Beg working in rounds, work 2(2.5:2.5)cms (¾:1:1in) in K2, P2 rib.
Cast off loosely in rib.

Armhole ribbing

With right side of work facing, using base col and 2¾mm (no. 12) needles, pick up and K7(8:9) sts from left holder,
Pick up and K63(66:69) sts to shoulder, 63(66:69) sts down to holder, 7(8:9) sts from holder. (140:148:156 sts). Place marker here to mark end of round.
Beg working in rounds in K2, P2 rib. Work for 2.5cm (1in).
Cast off loosely in rib.

Lady's Hat, Scarf and Mittens

Shetland 2-ply jumper yarn
beige (202): base colour, moorit (4), blue (FC15), dark
blue (21), cream (1a), yellow (28), rust (32).

Size
Average fit.

Repeats
A = 6 sts B = 12 sts C = (1st row of pattern) 26 sts 2 rows of plain base colour between bands of patterning

Materials
11ozs beige (202); 1oz moorit (4); 3ozs blue (FC15); 1oz dark blue (21); 1oz cream (1a); 1oz yellow (28); 1oz rust (32).
Sets of 3¼mm, 3mm, 2¾mm, 2¼mm (nos 10, 11, 12, 13) double-ended needles.
1 stitch holder.

Tension
9 sts to 1in on no. 11 needles and over patterning.
9 sts to 1in on no. 12 needles and over plain unpatterned st st.

Instructions
Using 2¾mm (no. 12) needles and base col, cast on 45 sts work 2ins in plain st st. Change to 3mm (no. 11) needles and work 3ins in Fair Isle patterning. Change to 2¾mm (no. 12) needles and work a further 2ins in plain st st. Cast off.

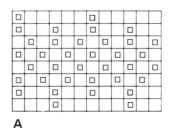

- ■ Moorit (4)
- ☐ Blue (FC15)
- ◉ Ochre (28)
- ▲ Rust (38)
- ▪ Navy (21)
- ☐ Beige (202) (base colour)
- ◎ Cream (1a)

A

B

- ▪ Blue (FC15)
- ☐ Beige (202)
- ∧ = sl I, K2 tog tbl, psso

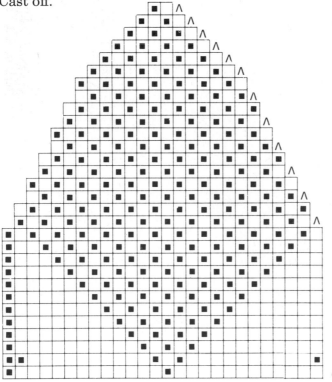

C

Your tension square should measure 7ins in length and 5ins across both plain and patterned rows. If your square measures more, use needles a size smaller than quoted, if your square measures less, use needles a size larger.

Mittens

Note: when working patterning it is advisable to weave in spare yarn on every stitch.

Right mitten: Using base col and $2\frac{1}{4}$mm (no. 13) needles cast on 36 sts on to 1st needle and 36 sts on to 2nd needle. (72 sts). With 3rd needle beg working in rounds of K2, P2, rib. Work 8.5cm ($3\frac{1}{4}$ins). Work 10 rounds in plain st st (every round K).

Change to $2\frac{3}{4}$mm (no. 12) needles and work pattern A and 7 rounds plain st st. Change to 3mm (no. 11) needles and work 4 rounds of pattern B.

** *5th round:* (cont working pattern as set in chart.) K40 sts, place next 12 sts on holder, return to right hand needle and cast on 12 sts. Work rem 20 sts to end of round ***. Complete pattern B. Change to $2\frac{3}{4}$mm (no. 12) needles and work 7 rounds plain st st. Change to 3mm (no. 11) needles and work pattern A. Change to $2\frac{3}{4}$mm (no. 12) needles and work 14 rounds plain st st.

Shape top:

1st round: * K2, sl 1, K1, psso, K28, K2 tog, K2. Rep from * to end of round.

2nd round: K.

3rd round: * K2, sl 1, K1, psso, K26, K2, tog, K2. Rep from * to end of round.

4th round: K.

5th round: * K2, sl 1, K1, psso, K24, K2 tog, K2. Rep from * to end of round.

6th round: K.

7th round: * K2, sl 1, K1, psso, K22, K2 tog, K2. Rep from * to end of round.

8th round: * K2, sl 1, K1, psso, K20, K2 tog, K2. Rep from * to end of round.

9th round: * K2, sl 1, K1, psso, K18, K2 tog, K2. Rep from * to end of round.

10th round: * K2, sl 1, K1, psso, K16, K2 tog, K2. Rep from * to end of round.

11th round: * K2, sl 1, K1, psso, K14, K2 tog, K2. Rep from * to end of round.

12th round: * K2, sl 1, K1, psso, K12, K2 tog, K2. Rep from * to end of round. (36 sts).

Graft together 18 sts on 1st needle and 18 sts on 2nd

needle (see p. 24).

Thumb: With 1st 3mm (no. 11) needle, pick up 12 sts from holder, with 2nd needle pick up and knit 12 sts from cast on sts at base of thumb. (24 sts). With 3rd needle beg working in rounds with 5th row of pattern B. Complete pattern B, change to $2\frac{3}{4}$mm (no. 12) needles and work 7 rounds plain st st. Change to 3mm (no. 11) needles and work pattern A. Change to $2\frac{3}{4}$mm (no. 12) needles and work 1 round plain st st.

Shape top:

1st round: (K1, K2 tog) 8 times. (16 sts).

2nd round: (K2 tog) 8 times. 8 sts.

Break off yarn, thread through remaining sts, fasten off and darn in end on wrong side of work.

Left mitten: Work as for right mitten to **.

5th round: (cont working pattern as set in chart) K20 sts, place next 12 sts on holder, return to right hand needle and cast on 12 sts, work rem 40 sts to end of round. Work as for right mitten from *** to end.

Hat: Using base col and $2\frac{3}{4}$mm (no. 12) needles cast on 78 sts on 1st needle. With 2nd needle, cast on a further 78 sts. (156 sts). With 3rd needle beg working in rounds of K2, P2 rib. Cont until work measures 13cm (5ins). Change to 3mm (no. 11) needles and work 5 rounds st st (every round K). Change to $3\frac{1}{4}$mm (no. 10) needles, work pattern A, 2 rounds base col, pattern B, 2 rounds base col, pattern C. (Work crown shaping as shown in chart, beg dec on 13th round). Work until 12 sts rem. Draw both strands of yarn through sts, secure to wrong side of work. Darn in ends.

Scarf: Using base colour and 1st 3mm (no. 11) needle, cast on 66 sts. Cast on 66 sts on 2nd needle. (132 sts). With 3rd needle beg working in rounds. Work 1 round, K2, P2 rib beg with K2. Work 5 rounds of ribbing as set. Work 8 rounds in base col and is st st (every round K). Change to $3\frac{1}{4}$mm (no. 10) needles and work patterns A, B and A with 6 rounds plain base col between each. Change to 3mm (no. 11) needles and work 107cm (42 ins) in base colour and in st st. Change to $3\frac{1}{4}$mm (no. 10) needles and work patterns A, B and A with 6 rounds plain base col between each pattern. Change to 3mm (no. 11) needles and work 8 rounds in base col and st st. Work 5 rounds K2, P2 rib. Cast off in rib. Make tassels and attach to both back and front lower edges of ribbing, keeping the side 'seams' straight, and so closing 'tube'.

Lady's Jacket

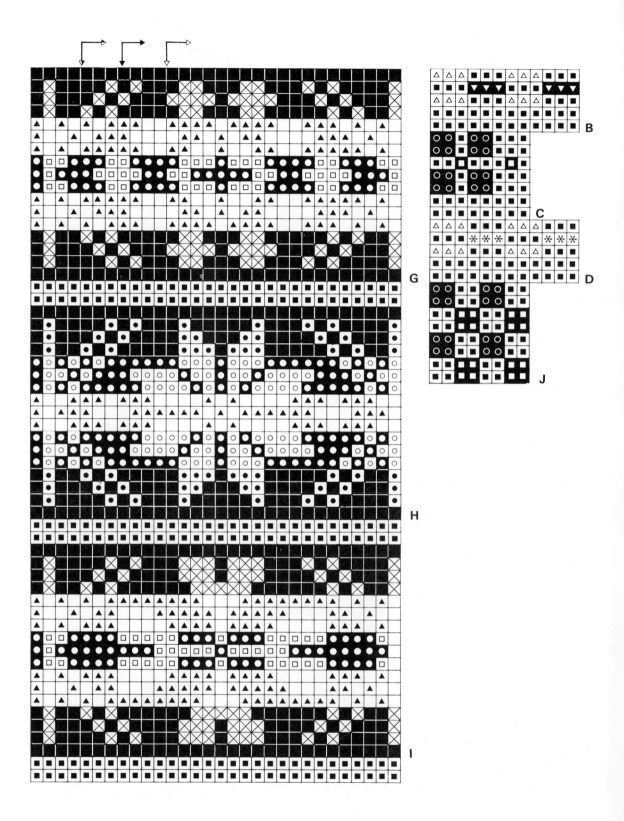

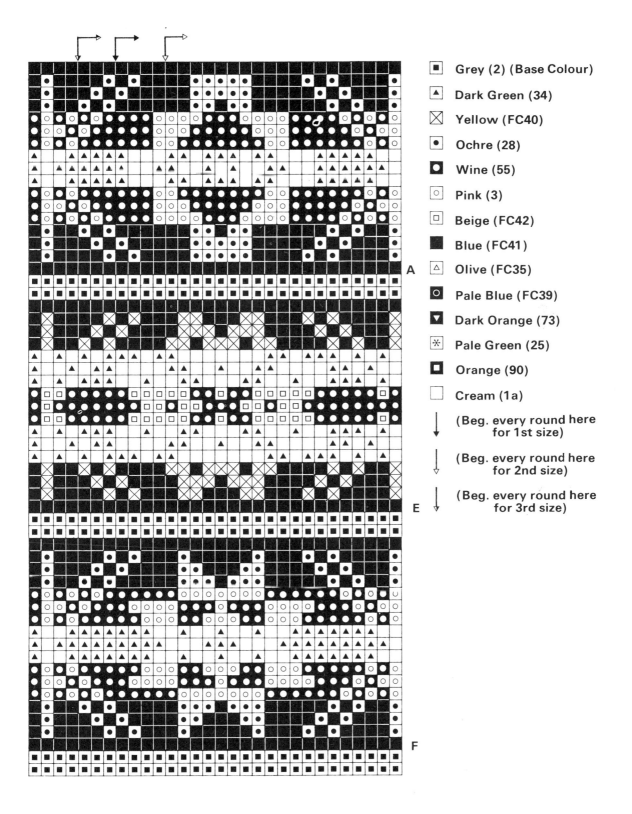

	Grey (2) (Base Colour)
▲	Dark Green (34)
⊠	Yellow (FC40)
●	Ochre (28)
◉	Wine (55)
○	Pink (3)
☐	Beige (FC42)
■	Blue (FC41)
△	Olive (FC35)
◉	Pale Blue (FC39)
▼	Dark Orange (73)
✳	Pale Green (25)
◻	Orange (90)
☐	Cream (1a)

↓ (Beg. every round here for 1st size)

↓ (Beg. every round here for 2nd size)

↓ (Beg. every round here for 3rd size)

A

E

F

Shetland 2-ply jumper yarn

grey (2), ochre (28), green (25), orange (90), dark orange (73), green (34), wine (55), cream (1a), pink (3), blue (FC41), yellow (FC40), beige (FC42), pale blue (FC39), pale brown (FC35).

Repeats

A 30 sts; B 6 sts; C 8 sts; D 6 sts; E 30 sts; F 30 sts; G 30 sts; H 30 sts; I 30 sts; J 4 sts.

Pattern order

D, A, B, C, D, E, B, C, D, F, B, C, D, G, B, C, D, H, B, C, D, I, B, C.
2 rows in base colour between each band of patterning.

Sizes

Actual sizes: 92(98:103)cms (36.3:38.6:40.6ins).

Materials

Shetland 2-ply jumper yarn: 6:6:8ozs grey (2); 1:1:2ozs ochre (28); 1oz green (25); 2ozs orange (90); 1oz dark orange (73); 2:2:3ozs green (34); 2:2:3ozs wine (55); 2ozs cream (1a); 1:1:2ozs pink (3); 3:3:4ozs blue (FC41); 2ozs yellow (FC40); 1oz biege (FC42); 2ozs pale blue (FC39); 1oz pale brown (FC35).
It would be helpful to order a colour card to identify the different wools.
2 short $2\frac{3}{4}$mm (no.12) needles,
3 41cm (16ins) $3\frac{1}{4}$mm (no. 10) double-ended needles,
3 41cm (16ins) 3mm (no. 11) double-ended needles,
3 41cm (16ins) $2\frac{3}{4}$mm (no. 12) double-ended needles,
or: $3\frac{1}{4}$mm, 3mm and $2\frac{3}{4}$mm (nos 10, 11, and 12) twin pins plus 3 $3\frac{1}{4}$mm, 3mm, $2\frac{3}{4}$mm (nos 10, 11 and 12) 30.5cm (12ins) double-ended needles.
8 stitch holders.
8 buttons, if desired.
2yds of 2.5cm (1in) wide petersham ribbon.

Tension

8.4 sts to 2.5cm (1in) on $3\frac{1}{4}$mm (no. 10) needles over patterning,
8.4 sts to 2.5cm (1in) on 3mm (no. 11) needles over plain st st,
9 sts to 2.5cm (1in) on 3mm (no. 11) needles over patterning (used for button bands and hem of pockets).
3mm (no. 11) needles must be used on all plain unpatterned rows/rounds between bands of patterning.

Instructions

Using 3mm (no. 11) needles and base col, cast on 42 sts. Work 2in in plain st st. Change to $3\frac{1}{4}$mm (no. 10) needles and work 3ins. in Fair Isle patterning. Change to 3mm (no. 11) needles and work a further 2ins in base col only and in plain st st. Cast off.

Your tension square should measure 7ins in length and 5ins across both plain and patterned rows. If your square measures more, use needles a size smaller than quoted, if your square measures less, use needles a size larger.

With base col and $2\frac{3}{4}$mm (no. 12) needles, or twin pin, cast on 72(77:81) sts onto 1st needle (for twin pin place marker for sideseam), 144(154:162) sts onto 2nd needle (for twin pin place 2nd marker for sideseam), 72(77:81) sts onto 3rd needle or twin pin. (288(308:324) sts.)

Wrap yarn 10 times round 3rd needle after last cast-on st for front opening. (Rep this procedure with every colour in use on each round.) For twin pin, work in rows turning at end of each row at centre front opening.

Beg working in rounds, knitting 1st st on 1st needle onto 3rd needle.

Work three rounds in garter st (1st round P, 2nd round K, 3rd round P).

Change to 3mm (no. 11) needles and work 2 rounds in st st and base colour (every round K).

Change to $3\frac{1}{4}$mm (no. 10) needles and beg patterning in st st. Work 16 rounds in pattern J. Cont working patterns as set until work measures 15cm (6ins) from beg.

Pockets

The opening for the pockets is made by knitting 36 sts for each in a length of contrasting yarn, leaving long loops of the colours used for the rest of the round hanging behind the pocket sts to be cut and sewn in later. (The pockets are knitted last.)

1st round: K10(12:14), K36 in contrasting yarn, K to last 46(48:50) sts, K36 in contrasting yarn, K10(12:14) to end.

2nd round: As normal, working over sts in contrasting yarn.

Cont without shaping until work measures 40.5(51:51)cms, (16:20:20ins) from beg.

Divide for front and back

K57(60:62) for right front. K10(12:14), place on holder for sleeve. K10(12:14) and place on another holder for sleeve, K134(140:144) sts and leave on holders for back, K10(12:14) and place on holder for sleeve, K10(12:14) and place on another holder for sleeve. K57(60:62) for left front.

Fronts

Cont on the 2 sets of sts for right and left fronts, working on 2 needles only and in rows. Cont to wrap yarns in use, on every row, round the needle to form opening at centre. For twin pin work right and left front separately using the same instructions below.

Dec 1 st at neck edges only on every 4th row until 45(48:50) sts rem on right *and* left front.

Cont without further shaping until work measures 23(25.5:25.5)cms (9:10:10ins) from base of armhole.

Leave sts on holder for shoulder.

Back

Rejoin yarn to 134(140:144) sts for back. Cont in st st on 2 needles and in rows until work measures 19(20.5:20.5)cms ($7\frac{1}{2}$:8:8ins) from base of armhole. End with a P row.

Next row: K53(56:58), cast off next 28 sts. K53(56:58) to end. Cont on these last sts for left back.

* Dec 1 st at neck edge only on next 8 rows. 45(48:50) sts. Cont without shaping until work measures same as front.

Leave sts on holder.

Rejoin yarn to sts for right back and rep as from * to end.

Graft shoulder seam (see p. 24)

(see p. 24)

Sleeves

With right side facing, using base col and 3mm (no. 11) needles, with 1st needle pick up and K10(12:14) sts from left holder aand 75(83:84) to top shoulder. With 2nd needle pick up and K75(83:84) sts from top of shoulder to 2nd holder. Pick up and K10(12:14) sts from holder. (170(190:196) sts).

Place marker at end of round for sleeve seam.

Work 2 rounds in base col. Beg. patterning and gusset shaping. Change to $3\frac{1}{4}$mm (no. 10) needles.

3rd size only
Next round: K12, sl 1, K2 tog, psso, K to last 15 sts, sl 1, K2 tog, psso, K12 to end.
Next round: K.

2nd and 3rd sizes only
Next round: K10, sl 1, K2 tog, psso, K to last 13 sts, sl 1, K2 tog, psso, K10 to end.
Next round: K.

All sizes
1st round: K8, sl 1, K2 tog, psso, K to last 11 sts, sl 1, K2 tog, psso, K8 to end.
2nd round: K.
3rd round: K6, sl 1, K2 tog, psso, K to last 9 sts, sl 1, K2 tog, psso, K6 to end.
4th round: K.
5th round: K4, sl 1, K2 tog, psso, K to last 7 sts, sl 1, K2 tog, psso, K4 to end.
6th round: K.
7th round: K2, sl 1, K2 tog, psso, K to last 5 sts, sl 1, K2 tog, psso, K2 to end. (154(170:172) sts).
8th round: K.
Rep last 2 rounds 5(7:6) times more. (134(142:148) sts).
Dec 1 st at the beg and end of every foll 5th round until 84(86:88) sts remain.
Cont without shaping until work measures 40.5(43:46)cms (16:17:18ins) from top of shoulder. (Check here for length.)
Work 2 rounds in base colour.
Work 12 rounds in check pattern.
Change to 2¾mm (no. 12) needles.
K 1 round in base colour.
P 1 round in base colour.
Cast off knitwise.

Button band
Cut and sew in the loops dividing the right and left front. Lay jacket flat and measure from the base of the hem at centre front opening around to centre back of neck, to one decimal point. Multiply this number by the number of stitches to the inch (on 3mm (no. 11) needles this should be 9). This will give you the number of sts to be cast on for each button band. Cast on the required number of stitches using the base colour and 3mm (no. 11) needles.
1st row: K (right side).

2nd row: Beg check pattern (J), work in st st beg with a P row.

Work 10 rows.

P 1 row in base colour.

Cast off knitwise.

Make second band as the first.

Sew band to front opening, using cast on edge to emphasize seam. Join centre back seam of band.

Sew petersham ribbon to band (2.5cm) wide, using cast on and cast off edges to emphasize sewing lines.

Pockets

Remove contrasting yarn knitted into fabric for pocket opening.

Place 36 sts from bottom row onto needle. Place 36 sts from top row on to holder.

With right side of work facing, using base colour and 2 3mm (no. 11) needles, work 6 rows check pattern in st st. Cont in base colour only.

Work 1 row in garter st.

Work 20.5cms (8ins) in st st. Graft these sts to those on holder (see p. 24).

With right sides together sew side seams of pockets.

List of Suppliers

Steel double-ended needles in various lengths
Stove and Smith,
98 Commercial Street,
Lerwick,
Shetland.

Leather knitting belts
Goodlad and Goodlad,
90 Commercial Street,
Lerwick,
Shetland.

Shetland 2-ply Jumper Yarn
Jamiesons Knitwear,
93–95 Commercial Street,
Lerwick,
Shetland.

Jamieson and Smith,
North Road,
Lerwick,
Shetland.